I0486648

Six Questions

Russell McGuire

Published by SDG Strategy, LLC, 2020.

SIX QUESTIONS

First edition. December 25, 2020.

ISBN: 978-1393015925

Written by Russell McGuire.

Table of Contents

Six Questions

Whenever I sit down with a business leader for the first time, I typically start by asking them to "tell me about your business". As they respond, I'll often gently probe for more details. When I first started doing this, it was a somewhat intuitive process, but over the years I have formulated it down to six questions that I'm hoping to get answered:

1. Why does the business exist?
2. What principles will the leaders never compromise?
3. Whom do they serve?
4. Why do customers choose them?
5. How do they make money?
6. What do they need to do right now?

. . . .

IN THIS INTRODUCTORY chapter I want to briefly introduce these six questions and then, through the remaining chapters, I want to dig more deeply into each of these areas.

My definition of strategy is "a framework that makes hard decisions easier." These six questions are an example of a business strategy framework. If you deeply understand the answers to these six questions then, when faced with a hard decision, testing the options against their alignment with and impact to these questions will help guide you to the right answer.

Throughout this book we will dive deep into these six questions and explore what you can do to be able to answer them well, but for now, let's make sure we have at least a high level understanding of what I mean by each of these.

Why does your business exist?

THIS QUESTION BASICALLY identifies the business' purpose or mission.

But when I'm talking to entrepreneurs, I also want to know their story. Why did they start the business in the first place? Why are you doing this? Startups are hard and require personal sacrifice. What was it that made you abandon what you were doing before to pursue this "crazy idea"?

What principles will you never compromise?

SOME COMPANIES CODIFY a set of "core values", but even many of the companies that do have not taken this concept seriously. This is one of the areas that makes many decisions hard: Logically, the best option is A, but that just doesn't "feel right".

Figuring out what really matters to you is really important. Making sure all the leaders on your team share those principles is even more important.

Whom do you serve?

THIS QUESTION IS MORE typically asked as "who is your target market?" And that certainly is part of what I'm looking for when I ask this question. But I also want to know about the people, the individuals that are benefitting from what you do.

Framing the question the way I have also forces the leaders to think rightly about their relationship with their customers. It may even cause them to realize that they have allowed their targeting to stray from why they started the business in the first place. If that alignment is broken, something needs to change.

Why do customers choose your business?

AGAIN, THE TYPICAL way to ask this question is "what is your differentiation?" Unfortunately, for many businesses the way they'd answer the question will differ depending on how it is asked.

Sometimes a business has worked hard to try to establish a certain basis for their differentiation — which may be unique features or capabilities, may be based on a geography or market they uniquely serve, or may be based on pricing, but in reality, customers are choosing them for an entirely different reason. If that's the case, then there's important work to be done.

How do you make money?

THIS IS THE "BUSINESS model" question. As phrased, I expect the leader to respond either in terms of where their revenue comes from, or how they manage the business to achieve profitability.

Eventually, I want to understand both sets of answers, but which of those the leader focuses on says a lot as well.

What do you need to do right now?

AT TIMES IN THE PAST, I would phrase this as "what are your strategic imperatives?" As a strategy guy, that sounds much more impressive and focused on strategic objectives.

But in reality, sometimes the things the business needs to do right now have more to do with survival than strategy. But how the business chooses to pursue survival needs to be aligned with the strategy (everything we've talked about above) if the business hopes to thrive in the long term.

When do the answers change?

QUESTIONS 1 AND 2 WILL probably never significantly change for a given business. They may be refined over time, but if question 1 changes then you basically have a new business.

Questions 3, 4, and 5 hopefully don't change very often. Sometimes there are external forces (opportunities or threats) that require focusing on different markets. Sometimes the competitive environment changes that leads to a different basis for differentiation. And sometimes significant industry disruption requires a new business model. But most likely, those changes are rare and involve major strategic planning efforts.

Question 6, on the other hand, is always changing. At least once a year, every business should reassess their plans and make sure their priorities are aligned with the current business realities and their strategy.

• • • •

SO IF IT'S SO IMPORTANT to get these answers right, then how do you do it? Read on!

Why Does This Business Exist?

In his 2009 TED talk[1], Simon Sinek argues that people make decisions, not based on rational understanding, but on emotional response to what they believe. He uses Apple Computer, the Wright Brothers, and Martin Luther King, Jr. as examples of success driven by leaders who start with "why".

In Sinek's model, businesses manage and communicate around a three tier hierarchy. At the center of his model is why the business exists. The next layer out is how they operate. The outer layer is what they do. Dell Computer makes computers that are sophisticated and technologically advanced. Dell markets themselves that way (starting with the "what") and someone making a rational decision could very easily choose to buy one of their products. Apple, on the other hand, starts with "We believe in challenging the status quo. We think differently" (why). "The way we challenge that status quo is by making our products beautifully designed, simple to use, and user friendly" (how). "We happen to make computers" (what).

When you define your business by why you do what you do rather than by what you sell, everything else starts to fall into place. When team members understand the why, they naturally will make decisions aligned with the why, even in the face of significant ambiguity and uncertainty. When customers understand your why, those that select you will more highly value your products and services and likely will be more loyal.

When you don't understand your why, everything can quickly fall apart. Decisions become hard, take too long, and involve too many people. Customers are fickle, willing to switch for the smallest reason. Employees feel little attachment to their jobs.

---

1. https://www.ted.com/talks/simon_sinek_how_great_leaders_inspire_action

In their book, *Built to Last*[1], Jim Collins and Jerry Porras found that a company being more ideologically driven and less profit-driven than comparison companies was one of the clearest differences marking visionary companies that outperformed their peers. By ideologically driven, the authors mean that the company is driven by a core ideology which they define as a purpose and core values.

Collins and Porras provide helpful guidance in what makes for a good purpose statement: "When properly conceived, purpose is broad, fundamental, and enduring; a good purpose should serve to guide and inspire the organization for years, perhaps a century or more. ... Indeed, a visionary company continually pursues but never fully achieves or completes its purpose — like chasing the earth's horizon or pursuing a guiding star. ... [A] visionary company can, and usually does, evolve into exciting new business areas, yet remains guided by its core purpose."

They use Merck as an example. In 1935, George Merck II said "[We] are workers in industry who are genuinely inspired by the ideals of advancement of medical science, and of service to humanity." In 1991, Merck's CEO P. Roy Vagelos said "Above all, let's remember that our business success means victory against disease and help to humankind." The words may have slightly changed with the times, but the purpose remained true and consistent, and it drove hard decisions within the company. When Merck could not attract distributors or government funding for Mectizan, a cure for river blindness, the company decided to give the drug away for free to anyone who needed it. A million people suffered from the disease at the time.

In their book, Collins and Porras make the point that it often takes a few years for startups to create their fully-developed purpose, but I think it's important for even the youngest startup to have a strong sense of purpose. For entrepreneurs, I think there tends to be two different aspects to the question of why the startup exists. The first explains the problem the company is trying to solve. The second tells the story of why the entrepreneur has a passion for solving the problem. Over time, this initial purpose can become more broad and generalized as described in the Collins/Porras core ideology.

If you're struggling with how to develop a purpose statement, I've created a video tutorial[2] that might give you some ideas. In that tutorial, I reference the Mulago Foundation Eight Word Mission Statement[3] template. I think it works pretty well and it is simply:

- A verb
- A target population
- An outcome

Mulago works with social enterprises, but I think the approach can work for all kinds of startups. Here are examples they provide:

- Save kids' lives in Uganda.
- Rehabilitate coral reefs in the Western Pacific.
- Prevent maternal-child transmission of HIV in Africa.
- Get Zambian farmers out of poverty.

So, what is your why?

2.　https://medium.com/clearpurpose/whiteboard-tutorial-purpose-statements-deaa51e8d027

3.　https://mulagofoundation.org/stuff/the-eight-word-mission-statement

Non-Negotiable Principles

The second of the six questions that I believe every business needs to answer is "What principles will the leaders never compromise?" Many businesses develop a list of Core Values to try to reflect what is important to them. Core Values can shape company culture and influence decision making at all levels of the organization.

We have been told that having such Core Values are essential to business success, and so we dutifully brainstorm a list that we can all nod our heads to, that will make employees feel good and customers feel comfortable doing business with us. Unfortunately, I fear that most lists of Core Values fall far short of what is truly necessary.

In *Built to Last*[2], James Collins and Jerry Porras defined Core Values as "The organization's essential and enduring tenets — a small set of general guiding principles; not to be confused with specific cultural or operating practices; not to be compromised for financial gain or short-term expediency." The authors emphasize that companies should have very few Core Values "for only a few values can be truly *core* — values so fundamental and deeply held that they will change or be compromised seldom, if ever."

Although Core Values may be a fairly recent term, the concept is not new. Collins and Porras quote from IBM CEO Thomas J. Watson writing in 1963, explaining how a corporation can sustain common cause and direction through leadership and market changes: "[I think the answer lies] in the power of what we call beliefs and the appeal these beliefs have for its people.... I firmly believe that any organization, in order to survive and achieve success, must have a sound set of beliefs on which it premises all its policies and actions. Next, I believe that the most important single factor in corporate success is faithful adherence to those beliefs."

In *Start With Why*[3], Simon Sinek naturally focuses first on a company's purpose, but he writes "Once you know WHY you do what you do, the question is HOW will you do it? HOWs are your values or principles that guide HOW to bring your cause to life." He argues that most companies develop their Core Values as a list of nouns: Integrity, Honesty, Innovation, Communication, etc., when they need to be verbs if they are to be effective. He gives as examples "always do the right thing" rather than "integrity" and "look at the problem from a different angle" rather than "innovation." "Articulating our values as verbs gives us a clear idea... we have a clear idea of how to act in any situation. We can hold each other accountable to measure them or even build incentives around them."

Unfortunately, I fear that Core Values often tend to be feel-good sentiments that don't really carry any authority and that are likely to change with new leadership or changing popular opinion. If that is what you want, you can do an Internet search for "business Core Values" and find articles such as "18 Core Company Values That Will Shape Your Culture & Inspire Your Employees[1]", "The 8 Values Every Company Should Live By[2]", and "The Three Core Values Powering A Successful Business[3]".

Rather than the generic term Core Values, I prefer the term Non-Negotiable Principles. What is needed is not a warm and fuzzy sense that the company has some desire to operate virtuously, but rather an unyielding commitment to principles that, when rightly understood, will help define what is unique about your business and will make many hard decisions easier.

Google's Ten Truths

EARLY IN THE LIFE OF Google, a small group of employees were asked to capture the company's culture. An engineer in the group summarized what everyone else was saying with the single phrase, "Don't Be Evil." The company's founders, Larry Page and Sergey Brin loved it and it became the company's motto. Page said "When you are making decisions, it causes you to think."[4]

Within a few years, that single phrase had been expanded to "ten things we know to be true.[4]"

1. Focus on the user and all else will follow.
2. It's best to do one thing really, really well.
3. Fast is better than slow.
4. Democracy on the web works.
5. You don't need to be at your desk to need an answer.
6. You can make money without doing evil.
7. There's always more information out there.
8. The need for information crosses all borders.
9. You can be serious without a suit.
10. Great just isn't good enough.

While not a perfect list, it's not hard to imagine how these foundational principles shape decision making at the company. But it's also easy to see how any list of guiding principles can become challenging, and the longer the list, the more likely conflicts will arise, leading to compromise.

For example, consider government censorship of Internet content.

The Internet arrived in China in 1994. By 1997, the government was starting to implement laws and technologies to limit the availability of information deemed dangerous by the communist

4.   https://www.google.com/about/philosophy.html

regime. In 1998, the government began the Great Firewall project which was completed in 2006. While some American companies provided technology used in the Great Firewall, others, including Google, objected and withdrew from the country. But a few years later the company introduced Google.cn, with a censored version of search results, to comply with government desires[5]. Is Google "focusing on the user" or is it "doing evil to make money"?

However, China is not the only country that requests that Google censor search results and the company often complies, including to requests from the U.S. government[5]. Remaining committed to non-negotiable principles can be hard.

Southwest Airlines' Promises

WHEN HERB KELLEHER and Rollin King were first starting Air Southwest in the late 1960s, they envisioned a different kind of airline with a unique culture. Early in the life of the company, that culture became known as The Southwest Way and was documented in a vision statement and a set of two promises[6].

The company's vision is: *To be the world's most loved, most efficient, and most profitable airline.*

The company's promise to employees is: *Southwest will provide a stable work environment with equal opportunity for learning and personal growth. Employees will be provided the same concern, respect, and caring attitude within the organization that they are expected to share externally with every Southwest Customer.*

And employees' promise to the company (and its customers) is: *I will demonstrate my Warrior Spirit by striving to be my best and never giving up. I will show my Servant's Heart by delivering Legendary*

5.   https://cs.stanford.edu/people/eroberts/cs201/projects/2010-11/ FreeExpressionVsSocialCohesion/google_policy.html

6. http://investors.southwest.com/our-company/purpose-vision-and-the-southwest-way

Customer Service and treating others with respect. I will express my Fun-LUVing Attitude by not taking myself too seriously and embracing my Southwest Family.

While not structured as typical Core Values, I do believe these statements reflect non-negotiable commitments to key principles:

- Customer Service
- Efficiency
- Fun

As the company has grown from a small airline with less than 200 employees serving just three cities in Texas to the third largest airline in the world (by passengers) with over 50,000 employees, it has remained committed to these principles[6] and I believe that commitment has led to the customer loyalty and profitability that have fueled the company's growth and success.

Let me encourage you to carefully and thoughtfully identify those principles that are non-negotiable for your business that will help make your hard decisions easier and that can help drive your success.

Whom Do You Serve?

The third of the six questions that I believe every business needs to answer is "Whom do you serve?"

As a consultant, one of the most common problems I encounter is a business trying to be "all things to all people." Sometimes the client doesn't even recognize that's what they are doing — they think they have defined themselves in a focused way, but when I start asking questions, it becomes clear that they are willing to help just about anyone with almost anything they need (within the broad scope of their business).

I've even caught myself doing it at times.

A fellow consultant explained it this way. If you are a professional athlete with a torn ACL, you don't want the family doctor down the street working on your knee, you want an orthopedic surgeon who has helped other professional athletes return to successful careers. On the other hand, if you are the mother of five young kids, you don't want an elite surgeon dealing with your son's sprained ankle, you want the family doctor down the street. Each doctor, by focusing on the right opportunities with the right patients will spend their marketing budgets well, will invest in the right capabilities and resources, and will build successful practices.

It's easy for a consultant to say "focus" but its much harder to do. I work with many startups, and when you're first starting, every dollar of potential revenue looks good.

I remember in my first startup having a hallway conversation with John, a neighbor in our office building. He needed a website and we built websites. I went to my co-founder David to talk about it. David said "Yeah, I talked to John too. His business isn't really a fit for us." I remember how upset I got and I think I brought our third co-founder into the discussion. In the end, David relented and tried to work with John on his website, but David was right. What John wanted didn't fit well with the way we worked. We spent much more time landing him as a customer and serving him as a customer than was justified by how much he was able to spend for his website.

That doesn't mean that you won't serve customers outside of your target market. You just don't spend resources trying to win those customers and you don't change your product or your service to uniquely meet their needs. If I'd let David explain to John the way we worked and how much it would cost, John would've deselected us. We probably would've even recommended to him someone better suited to his needs.

I believe that the question "whom do you serve?" needs to be answered at two levels.

You need to understand your target market — the broad grouping of customers on whom you're going to focus your marketing efforts. You need to deeply understand why this is the right market for your business — how the market's needs are aligned with your value proposition, why you can win against competitors, and whether it will provide favorable economics for your business.

But you also need to profile your target customer — the typical buyer of your product or service. You need to deeply understand how your offer fits with what they are trying to do, how they are hoping to create value, and what obstacles they have wrestled with in the past.

Know Your Market

ONE WEEKEND IN THE early 1980s while I was a freshman at the University of Florida my roommate and I drove down to Walt Disney World.

First we went to the Magic Kingdom. There were some rides we enjoyed, but mostly we were annoyed by the franticness of the happy young kids that filled the park. We weren't the target market for the Magic Kingdom.

Next we went to Epcot Center. There were some interesting exhibits, but mostly we were annoyed by the slowness of the "elderly" people who were stopping and taking pictures of every little scene. Again, we weren't the target market for Epcot.

We recognized that what Disney needed was a theme park for (easily annoyed) young adults like ourselves. In 1989, they finally opened the MGM-Disney Studios park and the Pleasure Island entertainment complex. (But by then we were no longer carefree college students in Florida.)

Very few product or service categories enjoy a homogenous market — one where almost everyone can be served with a single market approach (product, promotion, channels, price). Instead, it is critical for companies to properly segment the market, select which segments they will target, and develop appropriate market approaches for each segment. Failing to do so will result in a market approach that is very expensive (trying to reach and serve everyone) but that actually meets the needs of very few.

Market Segmentation

THE FIRST STEP IN THE process is to segment the market. A market segment is a distinct group of buyers who share a similar set of needs and wants.

The most obvious level of segmentation is between consumer and business customers. Marketing to consumers is very different from marketing to business decision makers and the approach to further segmentation differs significantly as well.

For consumers, Kotler and Keller identify four approaches to segmentation[7]: geographic, demographic, psychographic, and behavioral.

Geographic segmentation is pretty straightforward. Segments are identified by geography, whether that be at the regional or national level, or down to the neighborhood or postal code level, whatever is appropriate for determining the unique marketing mix (product, promotion, price, and distribution) for different segments. Local businesses often naturally serve a geographically defined segment. Consumers aren't likely to drive twenty miles to buy a gallon of gas, or order a gallon of gas from the other side of the world via the web or a mobile app.

Demographic segmentation has more dimensions of evaluation but still tends to be fairly straightforward. Demographic variables can include age, life stage, gender, income, generation, family life cycle, family size, race, religion, culture, education, nationality, and social class. For example, it seems that Disney's target market for the Magic Kingdom was middle-class American families with small children in the home.

Demographic segmentation is popular because market research is readily available to size these market segments, and these demographic factors often influence buyer behaviors and desires. While demographic segmentation can be very helpful in developing the best marketing mix for different segments, you have to be careful not to use demographic factors to discriminate *against* any protected classes.

Psychographic segmentation combines psychology and demographics to understand how consumers make decisions. One of the most popular psychographic classification systems is the VALS framework from Strategic Business Insights[1]. The VALS framework segments consumers into one of 8 mindsets based on two dimensions: primary motivations and resources. The primary motivators are ideals, achievement, and self-expression. Based on their primary decision making motivation, those with relatively low resources are categorized as Believers, Strivers, or Makers respectively. Those with relatively high resources are categorized as Thinkers, Achievers, and Experiencers respectively. The remaining two segments are outliers with Survivors being those with the lowest resources, and Innovators having high resources and exhibiting all three motivators to some extent.

Behavioral segmentation provides the most direct link between the consumer and the product by considering the consumer's needs and benefits, decision roles, and their use of the product (when, how, how much, loyalty, etc.). However, unlike the other approaches, information about the size and characteristics of behavioral segments can be much more difficult to obtain since this information is unique to each product category.

No matter what segmentation approach is used, it can be important to consider the different roles involved in the purchase decision. Often the purchaser is not the same as the user of the product and there often are other influencers involved.

---

1.   http://www.strategicbusinessinsights.com/vals/ustypes.shtml

For business markets, Kotler and Keller identify five sets of variables often used to segment the market: demographic, operating variables, purchasing approaches, situational factors, and personal characteristics. Companies will often use variables from across some or all of these areas in developing their segmentation.

Demographic segmentation for businesses tends to be much simpler than for consumers. Typical factors include industry, company size, and location.

Operating variables include technology, level of use, and customer capabilities.

Purchasing approaches include whether or not the business has a highly centralized purchasing function, who holds decision-making power (finance, engineering, etc.), purchasing criteria, general purchasing policies, and whether or not there's an existing relationship.

Situational factors include how urgently the customer needs the product, what their specific application is, and the size of order expected.

Personal characteristics include how similar the buying business is to the supplier, their attitude toward risk, and whether or not they show high loyalty to their suppliers.

Targeting

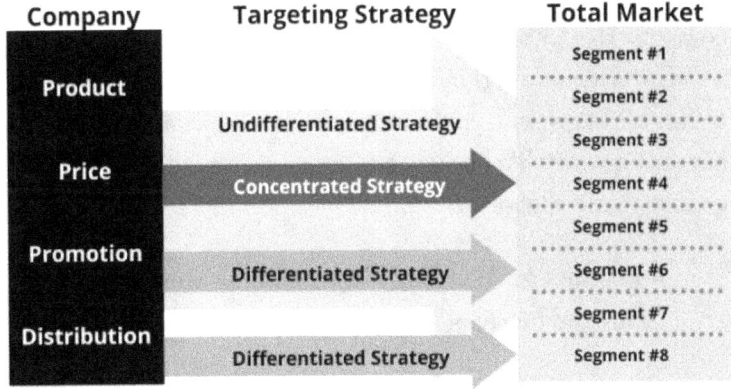

PRIDE AND FERRELL[8] outline three targeting strategies: undifferentiated, concentrated, and differentiated.

An undifferentiated strategy ignores market segmentation. It assumes that the entire market for a specific kind of product has the same needs and can be served with the same marketing mix (product, price, promotion, distribution). It is very rare for this to be the case, so, as I've mentioned above, this approach can be very expensive and is often very ineffective.

The concentrated strategy recognizes that segmentation makes sense and identifies a single segment to target. The company than designs a marketing mix for that one segment and focuses all of its resources on winning in that segment. This is the approach that almost always makes sense for startups with limited resources.

A company using a differentiated strategy similarly recognizes different needs and behaviors across segments, but unlike with the concentrated strategy, identifies multiple segments to target, each with their own marketing mix. A differentiated strategy takes more resources to pursue but increases the size of the addressable market and reduces the risk of being overly reliant on a single segment.

The differentiated strategy often grows out of the concentrated strategy. As a startup grows, increases its resources and capabilities, and builds the capacity to serve more customers, it is natural for the company to identify additional segments that can be targeted.

The critical question is how to choose which segment or segments to target? In general, you want to choose the segment(s) where you can have the greatest likelihood of success. I think there are four factors that go into that evaluation:

- **Product Market Fit:** How well does your offer meet the needs and behaviors of the segment?

- **Competitive Advantage:** Given other options being considered by potential customers, how likely are they to select you?

- **Financial Attractiveness:** How much will the segment spend on products like yours and how willing are they to pay a price that is profitable for you?

- **Long Term Attractiveness:** Is the segment growing or shrinking? Are there dynamics within the segment that are likely to change customers' needs or buying behaviors?

Sizing the Market

BLANK AND DORF[9] identify three ways that, especially startups, need to think about the size of the market they serve. The Total Addressable Market (TAM) is the amount that everyone spends for products in your category. The Served Available Market (SAM) looks only at the spend by those that you can serve through your distribution channel. Your Target Market is the total spend on products like yours by those in the segment(s) that you are targeting.

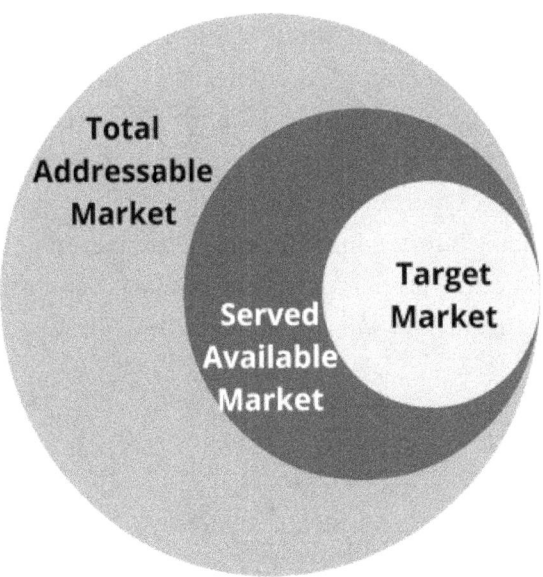

For example, you may be specifically targeting female action game players on the iPhone and naturally you are selling your action game through the iOS App Store. Your target market size would be the total spend by women on action games on the iPhone. The SAM would be the total spend on all action games through the iOS App Store (both men and women). The TAM could be either the total market for smartphone action games (including Android and other platforms) or perhaps even for all games across all smartphone platforms.

There are many market research firms that publish reports sizing the market for well established product categories. As Blank and Dorf note, these companies are "great at predicting the past." Their reports typically cost hundreds or thousands of dollars, and if you purchase reports on a single market from multiple research firms, you will typically find significant differences in their future projections. Furthermore, those reports usually won't segment the market the same way you have and so they may be able to provide an estimate for the TAM and possibly the SAM, but probably not for your Target Market.

With those qualifications, considering the market size estimates for the TAM and/or SAM from one or more research reports can be a better starting point for thinking about your target market than nothing. Often the research firms will issue a press release about each new research report and within the press release will be helpful total market sizing information. However, understanding the research firm's definition of the product category, the market, and their methodology for sizing the market will require purchasing the report.

Often startups are participating in creating new product categories or changing the business model for existing categories. In these cases, research reports won't help in sizing the market. Instead, a bottoms-up approach to market sizing is the best approach. You estimate the total number of buyers in your target market, how much/often they buy, and how much they are likely to pay given the new business model. Each of those three variables is a hypothesis that will need to be tested and refined over time, but you set your starting hypothesis from a deep understanding of the customers in the segment.

Know Your Customers

WHAT DOES IT MEAN TO understand your customer — your typical buyer? There are a number of different approaches to documenting knowledge of your customers.

One popular approach is to create one or more customer personas to bring what you know about your customers to life. Marketers often create a fictional character that represents their typical buyer. They give this persona a name (e.g. "Susan") and describe her as if she were a real person — for example what is her occupation, marital/family status, and age. What motivates her to buy your product? What frustrations inhibit her? Who influences her? Where does she shop? What TV shows does she watch? What magazines does she read? What websites does she visit? What other brands does she buy?

Where does this information come from? Some market research firms provide market segmentation with extensive information for developing a persona. For example, Experian sells the Mosaic USA[2] solution based on data for 126 American households. Experian segments households into 71 unique types within 19 groups (for example the "Golf Carts and Gourmets" type within the "Booming With Confidence" group). As their literature states, "A few clicks through the Mosaic portal, you'll be able to to discover the unique occupations, sources of entertainment, preferred means of advertising, enjoyed activities and other unique characteristics that make up each Mosaic group and type."

Online platforms like Facebook can also provide information about those interacting with your online ads. Surveying your own customers can also help in developing personas.

---

2.   https://www.experian.com/marketing-services/consumer-segmentation

Another popular approach, especially among startups, is to create a customer profile through the Customer Discovery process. In their book *Value Proposition Design*, Alex Osterwalder and team describe this profile as "the set of customer characteristics that you assume, observe, and verify in the market."[10]

In the Value Proposition Canvas, the customer profile breaks the customer down into his jobs, pains, and gains. Customer jobs "describe what customers are trying to get done in their work and in their lives"[11]. Gains describe what benefits the customer hopes to gain by doing the jobs. Pains describe the obstacles, risks, and bad outcomes that make it hard or painful to do those jobs.

So, how do you develop a customer profile? Steve Blank and Bob Dorf describe the Customer Discovery process: "Only by moving away from the comforts of your conference room to truly engage with and listen to your customers can you learn in depth about their problems, product features they believe will solve those problems, and the process in their company for recommending, approving and purchasing products."[12] In other words, you talk to and observe real customers to find out what they are really like and what they really need.

A Customer Discovery interview is very different from most business meetings. You aren't there to sell or even tell them about your product. You explain up front that you are there to learn about them, how they do what they do, and any problems they have that you might be able to help them solve in the long term.

The discussion can start as simply as "tell me about a typical day for you." You might need to guide them a bit to where they are talking about the aspect of their life or job that pertains to what your company does, but you don't want to force it. Part of what you want to learn is how important that aspect of their activity is relative to everything else they do.

When you get to the job or jobs they do that pertain to what your company offers, you want to ask questions like: "Why do you do that?" "What do you hope to get out of that?", and "What does it look like when that goes well?"

You can then ask whether or not it always goes well? If they say it does, then that is very important to know because it may mean that your opportunity to improve things is limited. Usually, though, they will have some level of dissatisfaction. Gauging the emotion behind their response can also signal how significant of an opportunity there is.

You should ask how they currently do that job and what they've tried in the past. For each thing they've tried ask "What worked well with that approach?" and "What didn't go so well?"

Another really good approach is to ask "Tell me about the last time you...[whatever problem your product helps them solve]". As they tell that story, you want to listen for what went well and what didn't, and probe further around those points using some of the questions above.

These types of discussions are critical for truly understanding your customers, what motivates them, and what problems they really want you to solve.

When you combine what you've learned about the target market and your customers, you can summarize it into this simple one-page view of whom you serve:

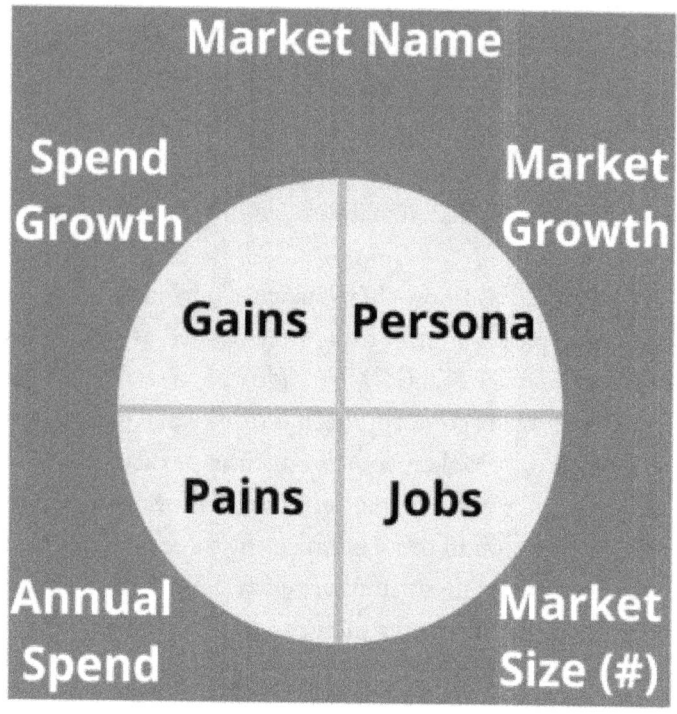

Why Do Customers Choose You?

T he fourth of the six questions that I believe every business needs
to answer is "Why do your customers choose you?"

If you've done a good job with Customer Discovery, as I described
in the previous chapter, then you'll have a good sense for what
motivates your target customers, how they dealt with their problem
before your solution came along, and what barriers you can help them
overcome. All of that is a great start to truly understanding why your
customers choose you.

Perhaps the most important question to start with is "who are my
competitors?" Too often when working with startups, I hear the answer
"we really don't have any competitors — no one is doing exactly what
we're doing." It may be good that no one is doing exactly what you're
doing, but it's foolish to think that you don't have any competitors. If
you are solving a real problem or meeting a real need, then your target
customers are already dealing with that problem/need somehow. At
the very least, the status quo is your competitor.

You have to understand who or what you are truly competing
against and what that competition's strengths and weaknesses are. It's
natural and okay for some customers to value your competitors'
solution better than yours. Understanding what makes your offer stand
apart is essential in how you target and qualify customers, how you
communicate your value proposition, and how you make decisions
about building and growing your business.

One of the questions that many businesses fail to ask is simply,
"what category do I belong in?" One of the companies I advise is
bringing a common everyday product into the modern age. Today,
people solve their problem with a cheap plastic solution that costs a
few dollars, but has significant limitations. My client's product is a
connected digital version of the product costing ten times the cost
of the original. If she positions her product in the same category as

her cheap, not-connected, plastic competitors then her product will be burdened with the same assumed shortcomings, but at an uncompetitive price. If, instead, she positions her product in the smart home category, then customers will automatically assign a completely different set of attributes to her product. Is that a good thing? Or does she need to create a new category for her product? These are really important questions.

Understanding your category and your specific competitors sets the stage for developing your unique competitive strategy. Michael Porter defined three generic competitive strategies and Treacy and Wiersema further characterized these generic strategies as market disciplines. Which one of those generic strategies makes sense for your business and how do you make it your own?

Finally, you need to clearly capture your value proposition. That value proposition will describe how your customers experience your product or offer in a way that they appreciate. But more importantly, that value proposition explains how your competitive strategy translates into specific activities that consistently result in that desired customer experience.

Who Are Your Competitors?

WHEN I HEAR A STARTUP leader say "we don't really have any competitors — no one else is doing what we do", that is a big red flag. It indicates one of two issues. Either the startup is targeting a problem not big enough to pursue, or the startup is naive enough to think that no one else is dealing with the problem they are addressing. For the purposes of this discussion, let's assume it's the latter.

Many startups are innovators. They are bringing new technology, business models, and/or operating models to bear in solving an existing problem. So, perhaps it's not surprising to hear "no one else is doing what we do."

But your competitors are not just other companies that have a product comparable to yours. You are competing with everything that your potential customer can use to deal with their problem.

If real customers really have the problem you are addressing, then they are already having to deal with it. Their current way of dealing with it may be a patched together collection of imperfect partial solutions (some bought, some borrowed, some home built), but whatever they are currently doing is your biggest competitor. Even the worst existing solution has the advantage of incumbency — the investment (in money and time) has already been made to put it in place and your potential customer may be thinking "if it ain't broke, don't fix it." So, competitor #1 is always the status quo, whether a competing company with a powerful product or a combination of spare parts held together with bailing wire, duct tape, and bubble gum. Never underestimate competitor #1.

But you wouldn't be chasing this opportunity if you didn't believe that at least some people were unhappy with the status quo. The next set of competitors you need to consider are those that, like you, are explicitly offering a better solution to the same problem. It may be true that no one is solving the problem the same way as you, but if the problem is worth solving then you can be sure that others are taking their own approach. Find them and learn everything you can about them.

Keep in mind that, when Southwest Airlines got started, they clearly competed with other airlines, but they also saw their new offer as competing with people driving themselves between cities, and by extension, they were competing with the railroad and bus lines. All those options were solutions to the problem of people wanting to go from Dallas to Houston.

The next group of competitors to identify are those that aren't (yet) explicitly trying to solve the same problem but who have what it takes to provide a solution. For example, how many problems being chased by software startups could actually be addressed by people using online Google Docs? Will Google create a new type of document for each of those opportunities? Probably not, but they could, and even if they don't they still represent an option for your potential customers.

You see, you aren't just competing against rivals specifically building products to solve the same problem as your product, but you are competing against every option your customers might consider for solving that problem.

Analyzing Competitors

MOST STARTUPS AREN'T naive enough to say that they have no competitors. Those that acknowledge their rivals will often respond to my question with a matrix that compares their solution to competitors. Typically the chart will have a column for the startup and one for each of their competitors. Down the left side will be a list of features or capabilities. The cells are filled with checkmarks and x's to highlight the shortcomings of competitors' offers.

	Us	Competitor A	Competitor B	Competitor C
< $100	✓	✗	✗	✓
Feature 1	✓	✓	✓	✓
Feature 2	✓	✗	✓	✗
Capability I	✓	✗	✗	✗
Capability II	✓	✓	✗	✗

This may not be a bad competitor analysis to use in a sales presentation with a potential customer. It focuses on the strengths of your offer and shows how competitors' offers don't share all of those strengths. However, once you start believing that this accurately reflects the threat level of your competitors, you're probably setting yourself up for an unpleasant surprise.

Instead of picking the features and capabilities on which you excel, you need to evaluate competitors on the factors that really matter as customers evaluate options to solve their problem. What are those factors? I can't tell you, but your potential customers can! And hopefully you've asked them.

Another diagram I often see is a variant on the perceptual map. This diagram picks two factors that are important to customers and plots competitor positioning against those two factors. Theoretically, the best solution is in the top right corner, and amazingly, every time a startup shows one of these maps they are in the top right!

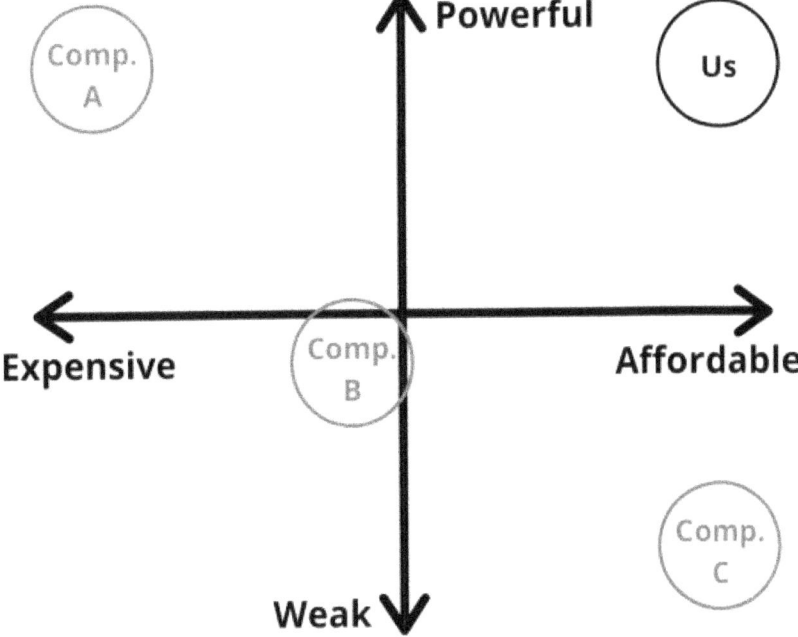

A much better tool for tracking competitors is the Strategy Canvas introduced by W. Chan Kim and Renée Mauborgne in *Blue Ocean Strategy*[13]. This tool shows the relative performance of competitors against the full list of competitive factors that matter to customers. The distinctions, both positive and negative, become quickly clear. In reality, some potential customers will prefer the mix of capabilities of your competitors over your unique mix. Being able to recognize those customers will help you qualify prospects and focus your attention where you have the best opportunity to win.

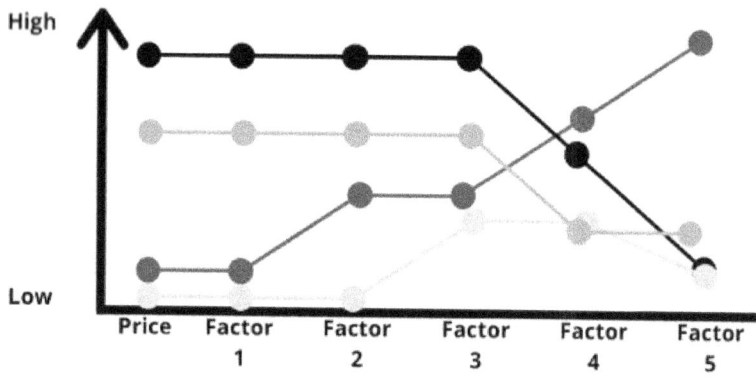

In addition to understanding the strengths and weaknesses of your competitors relative to customer decision factors, it's also very helpful to understand characteristics of each company that may not show up in the Strategy Canvas. Where are they based? What is their business strategy and their competitive strategy? How do they distribute their product? How deep are their resources (especially cash and people)? On which markets do they focus?

Once you've done all of that very important work, you'll be ready when I ask "who are your competitors?" The answer I love to hear is "what do you want to know?" When you've done your homework (and keep these competitor profiles always updated), then you are ready to tell me about direct, indirect, and even home-grown competitors. You can tell me what their strengths are today and what they can bring to bear to improve their position in the future. You can tell me when they win today and why you're concerned about their ability to win tomorrow.

What Category Are You In?

IN THE BIBLE, THE APOSTLE Paul wrote "Do not be deceived: 'Bad company ruins good morals.'"[14] Sometimes people assume certain things about us because of those with whom we are associated. Products can suffer the same fate.

Humans, by our nature, like to simplify the process of understanding products. When we hear of a new product, we want to put it into a category so that we can relate it to other products that are similar. The category provides a shortcut for our brain. We know that other products in that category have certain characteristics and we expect this new product to share those characteristics. We also have a sense for which attributes factor into our decision making process when evaluating options within that category.

For example, decades ago, if we'd heard there was a new brand of razor on the market, we might have been mildly interested. Razors, after all, lasted a very long time if you took good care of them. Some razors had replaceable blades and others had to be sharpened, but a good razor would be easy to hold and maneuver and would have a good solid feel so you could count on it to get the job done for decades.

But then Remington introduced electric razors that worked very differently. And then Bic introduced disposable razors. Although each of these types of razors solved the same problem as traditional razors, each had very different product attributes. Consumers first had to evaluate which category best met their needs, and then they had to choose a product within that category. If someone simply tried to evaluate a Remington or Bic razor using the normal evaluation criteria for a traditional razor, the new products would not fare well.

Remington and Bic had to work hard to educate consumers on the benefits of their new categories, but once consumers understood the significant benefits of each, the companies' dominance in their respective markets paid off handsomely. More importantly, if each had simply tried to compete in the existing category, they would've probably been seen as uncompetitive and likely would have failed.

Modern companies similarly benefit from introducing disruptive innovations and creating new product categories. According to a 2013 article in *Harvard Business Review*[15], from 2009–2011, 53% of revenue growth and 74% of incremental market capitalization growth amongst the 100 fastest growing companies in the U.S. came from new category creators.

That doesn't mean that every product can or should be made into its own category. Making a new category takes time and can be expensive. One nice thing about existing product categories is that they do much of the work in communicating value to consumers. By positioning within an existing category, a company can focus on marketing what is unique about their product and what sets them apart within that category.

Furthermore, companies that try to create a new category when one isn't justified often fail. At TeleChoice, we developed the category maker warning flag shown below.[16]

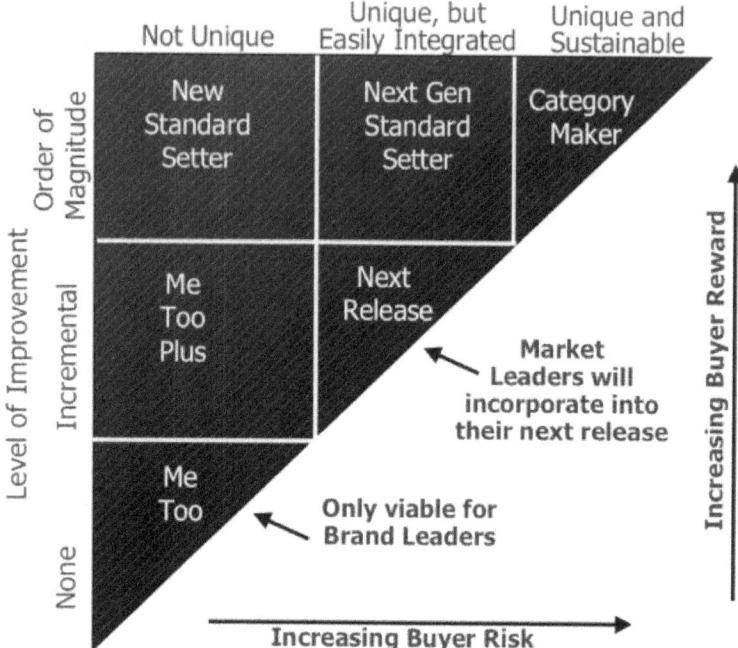

The flag captures five fundamental truths:

1. Valuable innovation creates meaningful improvements for customers.
2. Innovation that relies on a totally different approach is harder for existing competitors to replicate.
3. This level of innovation also represents the greatest risk for customers since they may have to change their own processes or habits. They also are being asked to "bet" on a relatively unproven new approach.
4. The bottom right half of the flag is missing because it's simply not viable. Customers won't take on significant risk unless there is meaningful benefit.
5. The opportunity to be a category maker really only exists for those with the highest level of innovation and the highest

level of benefit to buyers.

That being said, even if it doesn't make sense for a company to make a new category, everyone should work hard to ensure that their products are identified with the right categories in buyers minds.

Being in the right category makes it easy for buyers to understand the product and its value proposition and for the company to highlight the product's unique value. Being in the wrong category confuses buyers which means the company has to work that much harder to communicate their value proposition. The wrong buyers are initially attracted to the product, they compare the product to the wrong competitors, and they evaluate the product on the wrong criteria.

For example, the client I mentioned at the beginning of this chapter is developing a digitally connected product that protects children from dangerous situations in the home. The problem that her product solves is currently addressed by inexpensive plastic products that parents find hanging on a peg in WalMart.

Those competitive products are attractive because they are cheap and they provide peace of mind. But they are inconvenient, sometimes even painful to use so peace of mind can easily become "giving it a piece of my mind." And, since those competing products are simply pieces of plastic, it is impossible to check their status or change their status unless you are standing right in front of them, so that peace of mind can be quickly lost when leaving the kids with an easily distracted babysitter.

While my client wants buyers of those competitive products to know about her product, she doesn't want them to think of her digitally connected product as having the same attributes or to evaluate her product using the same criteria as they use for those competing products (primarily price). Instead, she wants them to think of her product as part of the category of smart home devices that consumers are increasingly using to protect their homes and families. Her product has attributes similar to wireless security cameras, smart door locks, and smart light bulbs. By aligning with this category, buyers will immediately understand the value that her product provides and will evaluate her product appropriately.

So, do you know why your customers choose you? The product category that you are aligned with has more to do with it than you might have imagined!

What Is Your Competitive Strategy?

POSITIONING AGAINST THE right competitors is important. Deeply understanding the strengths and weaknesses of those competitors is necessary for determining not only why customers choose you today, but how you can continue to win far into the future.

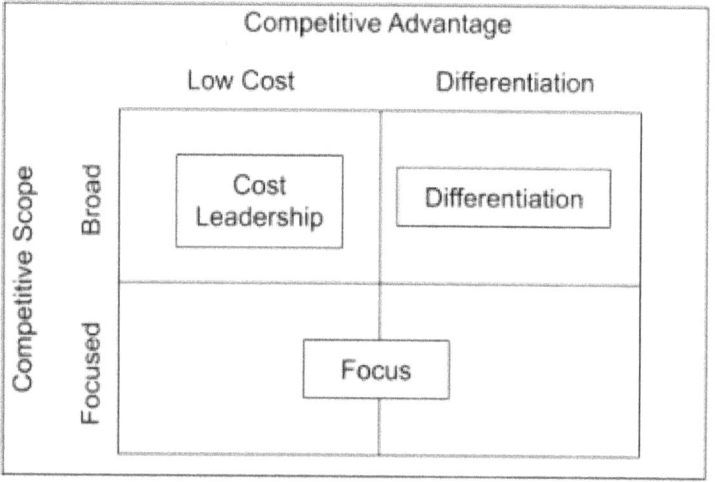

The classic framework for competitive strategy was published by Michael Porter in 1980[17]. He introduced three generic strategies: cost leadership, differentiation, and focus. Porter argued that it was critical for a business to choose one, or else they would get caught in the inherent tradeoffs between the different strategies.

While Porter speaks of three generic strategies, he defines these three using decisions along two different dimensions. The first decision is what Porter references as *competitive scope* — will the business compete broadly across the entire market, or will it focus on one or a few relatively narrow market segments. The second decision is what form of *competitive advantage* the business will pursue — a low-cost advantage or a differentiation advantage.

In their 1995 book *The Discipline of Market Leaders*[18], Michael Treacy and Fred Wiersema took Porter's model and described the three strategies using language a bit easier for managers to understand and apply.

In studying market leaders across many industries, the authors found that the companies clustered around three different "market disciplines" defined by the "kind of value proposition the companies pursued — best total cost, best product, or best total solution." They named these three disciplines operational excellence, product leadership (reflecting constant innovation), and customer intimacy (reflecting a deep understanding of specific customer needs), corresponding with Porter's cost leadership, differentiation, and focus strategies respectively.

Treacy and Wiersema make the point that, to be a leader, a business has to be "good enough" in all three disciplines, but will stand out in one of the disciplines. Companies that try to outperform in more than one discipline will struggle because of the conflicts that will arise when trying to make decisions.

While determining why you win today may be as easy as asking customers, determining your competitive strategy takes careful analysis and unflinching commitment.

Today, customers may be choosing your product because it has a lower price than competitors. But do you really have a sustainable cost advantage over competitors? Are you willing to consistently make decisions to maintain that cost advantage? Will you resist the temptation to chase expensive and unnecessary product innovation or customer-centric initiatives?

Or if it is a unique innovative product feature that sets you apart today, do you have the ability and resources to maintain that innovative product leadership in the future? Will you outspend competitors in research and development and are you committed to maintaining the agility necessary to rapidly bring new features to market?

If, instead, customers choose you because you have unique insight into their specific needs and deliver customized solutions just for them that your more generalist competitors can't match, are you willing to maintain that focus going forward? Will you invest in more deeply understanding your target customers and more compassionately serving them, while resisting the temptation to broaden the appeal of your offers with generic features? Are you willing to maintain a narrow market focus and not chase every customer and every market that you encounter?

Answering the question "why do customers choose you" needs to be answered not only for today, but with a long term commitment to a sustainable winning strategy.

What Is Your Value Proposition?

IN THIS CHAPTER WE'VE sought to answer the question "why do customers choose you?" We started by deeply understanding your customers and your competitors. Next we sought the right category for your product, and the right competitive strategy for your business. Now we need to bring all that together into a single sentence and a single diagram.

A company's value proposition is the reason that customers buy from you. It explains the tangible way in which you create value for your customers.

Many people are familiar with the Value Proposition Canvas[1] (VPC) first introduced by Alex Osterwalder and team in *Value Proposition Design*[19]. The VPC is a tool for understanding (and even developing) your value proposition for a specific customer segment. The VPC has two main components – a Customer Profile and a Value Map. The Customer Profile has three components – jobs, what customers are trying to get done in their work and their lives; gains, the outcomes and benefits they hope to get by doing those jobs; and, pains, bad outcomes, risks, and obstacles that often make it hard or impossible to achieve those gains. The Value Map similarly has three components – the products and services you offer; gain creators, the ways in which your delivery of those products and services help customers achieve their desired gains; and, pain relievers, the ways in which your delivery of products and services helps them overcomes the troublesome pains.

I've been a big fan of the VPC. It is an elegant and structured way to represent how a company creates value for a specific type of customer, but as I've used it with various teams over the past few years, I've struggled with a few aspects of the tool:

- Every time I use the VPC I start with the customer. You can't begin describing your value proposition without first understanding customer jobs, pains, and gains. However, the customer is on the right half of the VPC and English speakers naturally "read" a diagram left-to-right, so many new to the tool try to start with the value map instead of the customer.

- The Customer Profile aspect of the VPC does a great job of capturing the essential elements of the jobs, gains, and pains. But it really doesn't describe who the customers are.

• Similarly the Value Map aspect of the VPC does a great job of describing the core elements of the company's offer and how your specific way of providing that offer helps customers achieve their gains and overcome their pains. But what is missing is a sense of direction, or long-term focus to ensure that the offer will continue to successfully provide value to customers.

• Finally, what is most obviously missing from the VPC is a clear value proposition statement. The VPC was obviously designed to fit into the authors' earlier Business Model Canvas[2] (BMC). Specifically, it addresses the two parts of the BMC that I believe must be developed first — the customer/market and the value proposition. However, the BMC expects a statement of the value proposition in a form that the VPC simply doesn't deliver.

So, I've developed the Customer Value Map (CVM), which puts the customer first and adds three important elements:

• A Persona space for succinctly describing the target customers.

• A Market Discipline space for describing the long-term focus required to maintain competitive differentiation.

• A Product Positioning statement to capture, in sentence form, the core reason that the target customers will value the offer and choose it over other options.

Here's a representation of the CVM:

---

2. https://www.strategyzer.com/canvas/business-model-canvas

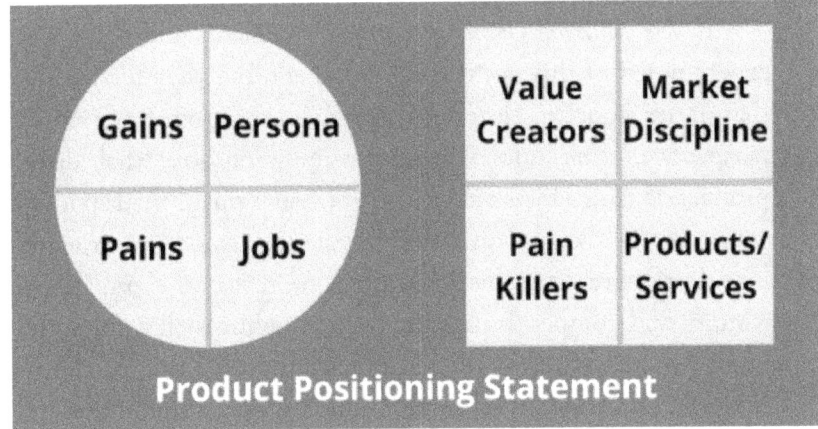

Gains | Persona — Value Creators | Market Discipline

Pains | Jobs — Pain Killers | Products/ Services

Product Positioning Statement

The Product Positioning Statement

BASED ON OUR PREVIOUS DISCUSSIONS ON understanding who buys from you, I think you can imagine the kinds of demographic, geographic, psychographic, and behavioral factors you can list under the new *persona* space to capture the essence of who you are selling to. Similarly, from our previous discussion about competitive strategy you should have a sense for what goes in the *market discipline* space.

The Product Positioning Statement, however, is something we haven't talked about yet.

In *The Strategy Focused Organization*[20], Kaplan and Norton expect the value proposition to carry a lot of weight: "The core of any business strategy — connecting a company's internal processes to improved outcomes with customers — is the 'value proposition' delivered to the customer. The value proposition describes the unique mix of product, price, service, relationship, and image that the provider offers its customers. The value proposition determines the market segments to which the strategy is targeted and how the organization will differentiate itself, in the targeted segments, relative to competition."

In *The Startup Owner's Manual*[21], Blank and Dorf similarly expect much of this positioning statement, but they further demand that it be concise, clear and compelling: "From your customer's perspective, what does your company stand for, what does your product do, and why should they care? You probably had an idea when you started the company, but now you have some real experience in interacting with customers. It's time to revisit the product vision, features and competitive information in light of what you've learned in customer discovery... In technology startups, one of the biggest challenges for engineers is to realize the need for a simple message that grabs customers' hearts and wallets, not their heads and calculators. It's not about the product features. Seek a simple sentence that condenses the entire value proposition into a few pithy, catchy words that say it all."

In the 1940s, advertising executive Rosser Reeves introduced the concept of a Universal Selling Proposition (USP), the unique benefit exhibited by a company or product that enables it to stand out from competitors. Reeves said that the USP must clearly communicate "buy this product, for this specific benefit" in a compelling way that can't be matched by rival options.

In *Crossing the Chasm*[22], Geoffrey Moore provided a simple template for starting the development of a product positioning statement:

> For *[target customer]* who *[statement of need]*, the *[product name]* is a *[product category]* that *[statement of key benefit]*. Unlike *[primary competitive alternative]*, our product *[statement of primary differentiation]*.

Starting from this generic form, you can tighten and focus the language into something concise and compelling for customers.

Examples of powerful product positioning statements include:

- "Melts in your mouth, not in your hand." M&Ms
- "When it absolutely, positively has to be there overnight." FedEx
- "The ultimate driving machine." BMW
- "Save money. Live better." Walmart

These are so concise and catchy that they work as taglines, but they also clearly communicate the unique value to customers and why they should buy from these companies.

Now, what is your answer to the question "why do customers choose you?"

How Do You Make Money?

The fifth of six questions that every business should be able to answer is "how do you make money?" When I ask leaders this question I typically hear one of two types of answers: where their revenue comes from, or how they manage to profitability. Both answers are really important and which one they give even tells me a lot about their business.

I think it's important to understand the difference between a *revenue model*, a *business model*, and a *cash flow model*.

Entrepreneurs are often asked "what is your *business model*?" In most cases, I think the one asking the question really wants to know the startup business' *revenue model*. Especially amongst tech startups, the term "business model" is often used to describe who pays and how they pay. The answer expected might be "we have a subscription-based model" or an "advertising-based model" or perhaps "ours is a two-sided platform model". But these don't really reflect an entire *business model*.

The simplest definition of a *business model* is "how a business makes money", but a more effective definition is "how a business creates value for its customers and captures value from its customers". In the previous chapter we explored the concept of the value proposition — this reflects the value being created for customers. Much of the business' activities are in support of that value proposition — creating products, delivering services, providing customer support, etc. so that the value proposition is realized. The *operating model* is the portion of the *business model* that describes all of the activities and resources involved in that value creation.

The *revenue model* is the portion of the *business model* that explains how the business captures value from its customers. It describes which customers receive the value, which customers pay for the value, and how they pay. So you can see that the "*business models*" described two paragraphs above are really only talking about the *revenue model* part of the complete *business model*.

In this chapter we will talk about *revenue models* and *business models*. It's important to think about where the revenue comes from, as well as the complete picture of the *business model* including the *revenue model* and the *operating model*.

Most importantly, it is critical to deeply understand how cash flows through the business. What upfront investments are required to establish the ability to deliver the value proposition? Where does that cash come from? What revenues are expected to be captured by delivering the value proposition? What does it cost to operate the business to deliver the value proposition? What cash is expected to be generated by the business model? How will that cash be used? What future investments are required? Will cash be used to repay investments (with returns)? What is the timing of all of this? In this chapter we will also talk about this *cash flow model* of the business.

And "how do you make money" sounded like such a simple question!

What Is Your Revenue Model?

DECIDING HOW MUCH TO charge whom for what is a big and important issue for any company to resolve. Determining when to get paid and in what form can strongly impact your revenue growth and even why and how people adopt your product.

Since revenue is the fuel that keeps the business engine running, getting these decisions right can be the difference between life and death for startups.

The revenue model defines how a business captures value from its customers.

In order to capture value, the business must create value for customers, which is reflected in the value proposition, which we discussed in the last chapter. In reality, many businesses will create multiple forms of value for different types of customers.

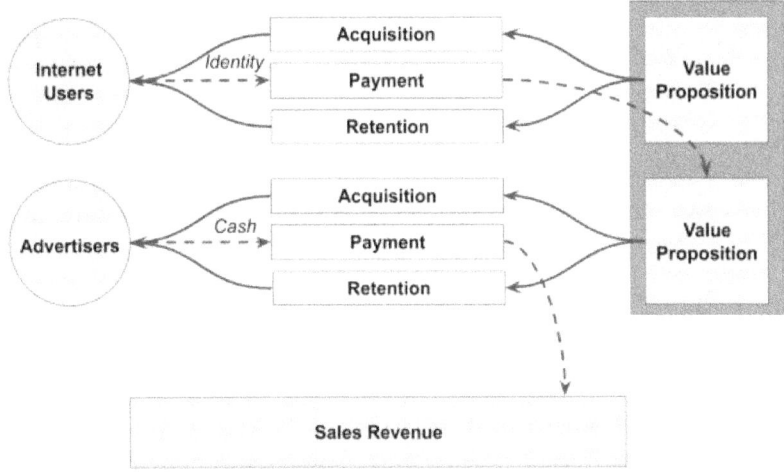

For example, Google makes it easy for Internet users to find information and it helps advertisers reach potential customers. The diagram below shows a simplified version of the revenue model for Google.

Let me briefly walk through the pieces here.

Google's value proposition to Internet Users is to make it easy for them to find information. Their brand strength and their success in delivering that value proposition are the primary means of acquiring and retaining these customers and the customers consume the value proposition through a variety of channels including Google's website, mobile app, and voice assistant devices. Customers "pay" for the service by implicitly allowing Google to identify them and to build a profile around their identity. That value then contributes directly to the value proposition for advertisers.

Google's value proposition to Advertisers is to connect them with potential customers. As above, their brand strength and success in delivering that value proposition are the primary means of acquiring and retaining customers. Google primarily delivers that value proposition through the Google Ads tools accessible through the Web and mobile apps and the customers make cash payments to Google through automatic and manual electronic payments established online. That cash counts towards Google's sales revenue and provides the bulk of the company's cash flow.

I think this one example gives a sense for the components of a revenue model. It reflects the relationship between the value proposition and the customer, how that customer is acquired and retained, the nature of the payments made by the customer, and how much of that is actual cash contributing to the cash flow of the business.

That makes it sound simple, but there are so many different possible variants that business have a very complex set of decisions to make. For example, payments can be made in advance of, or after experiencing the value provided. Payments can be one time, on a regular (monthly or annual) subscription period, or based on actual usage. Payments can be direct or through a third party. And the real and perceived value delivered can take many different forms.

Here is a quick summary of some different forms of revenue models:

- **Markup:** A good is sold to a buyer at a sales price above the item's cost in order to generate a profit.

- **Commission:** The value proposition is the mediation of a transaction between a buyer and a seller. The seller receives the purchase price but either the buyer or the seller pays the business a commission fee on the transaction.

• **Advertising:** The consumer of the primary product pays little or nothing, but agrees to receive targeted advertisements. The advertisers pay for access to the consumer.

• **Loss Leader Product:** The buyer purchases the primary product at an unprofitable price (sometimes free), but the business makes money on marked-up services or supplies necessary to continue using the product.

• **Rental:** The buyer pays to use a tangible product for a limited time but does not take ownership of the product.

• **Subscription:** The buyer pays to access an intangible (e.g. content or software) product or service for a specified time.

• **Licensing:** The buyer pays for the right to use an intangible product but does not technically own the product.

• **Barter:** The buyer and seller exchange non-cash products and services of value each to the other.

There are many other forms of revenue models, and each of these can take many different forms. But they all involve the same basic decisions to be made by the business in establishing how to offer the value proposition in a way that allows the business to capture the value and accomplish the business' objectives.

In addition to understanding how the business brings in revenue, it's essential to make sure that it can effectively create the value being offered.

What Is Your Business Model?

MY FAVORITE BOOK ON business models is *Business Model Generation*[23] by Alex Osterwalder and team. In the first few pages of that book, business models are defined in a few different ways. "A business model describes the rationale of how an organization creates, delivers, and captures value." "The business model is like a blueprint for a strategy to be implemented through organizational structures, processes, and systems." "We believe a business model can best be described through nine basic building blocks that show the logic of how a company intends to make money. The nine blocks cover the four main areas of a business: customers, offer, infrastructure, and financial viability."

Those nine blocks are communicated in the Business Model Canvas (BMC), which the book introduced:

Key Partners	Key Activities	Value Propositions	Customer Relationships	Customer Segments
	Key Resources		Channels	
Cost Structure		Revenue Streams		

When I first encountered the BMC, I thought it was a brilliant way to summarize an entire business on a single page. I still think that. But I'm not convinced it adequately describes a company's business model, at least not in a manner that is helpful for people using the tools to understand and develop real businesses. Others have adapted[1] the BMC to better meet the needs of LEAN startups, but I think we need to go a level deeper.

Another favorite book of mine is *Competing in the Age of AI*[24] by Marco Iansiti and Karim Lakhani. The book ultimately is about the business model innovation being enabled by the Connected Intelligence Revolution[2]. The authors introduce business models in this way: "The value of a firm is shaped by two concepts. The first is the firm's *business model*, defined as the way the firm promises to create and capture value. The second is the firm's *operating model*, defined as the way the firm delivers the value to its customers." Later they explain "Whereas the business model creates a goal for value creation and capture, the operating model is the plan to get it done."

Another helpful discussion of business models can be found in *Open Business Models*[25] by Henry Chesbrough. "At its heart, a business model performs two important functions: value creation and value capture. First, it defines a series of activities that will yield a new product or service in such a way that there is net value created throughout the various activities. Second, it captures value from a portion of those activities for the firm developing the model."

So, there seems to be pretty good consensus that a business model can be defined as "how a business *creates* value *for* its customers and *captures* value *from* its customers."

I have found it helpful as I work with teams, especially in the earliest stages of business conception and formation, to break the business model into these two main functions (value creation and value capture). The operating model is what I call the value creation portion of the business model. The revenue model is what I call the value capture portion. You may have slightly different definitions for those two terms, and that's okay.

---

1.   https://leanstack.com/leancanvas/

2.   https://medium.com/clearpurpose/the-connected-intelligence-revolution-a5fa32a654ea

We've already looked at the revenue model. Now we will consider the operating model. Together, they make up the business model.

The Operating Model

THE CHALLENGE WITH developing a generic template for an operating model is that operating models differ significantly depending on what business you are in. If you make products, a significant component of your operating model will be manufacturing. If you own and operate stores, a significant component of your operating model will be retailing. Whirlpool's operating model looks very different from Best Buy's operating model. Google's looks very different from either of them.

One aspect that I have greatly appreciated about the BMC has been the two blocks to the left of the value proposition: key resources and key activities. I would describe these two as "what you need" and "what you do" to deliver the value proposition. The remaining block on the left side of the BMC is key partners, which I typically describe as "who helps you complete the value proposition". While I like the conceptual structure of these three blocks, they are so broad and so generic that I don't know that they really help in developing a business.

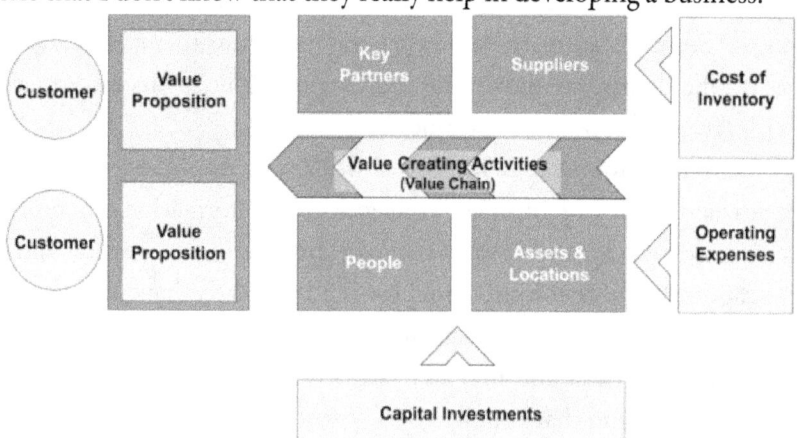

Here is my Operating Model template.

As I did with the value proposition and the revenue model, I've reversed the direction compared to the Business Model Canvas. (You might reference the BMC diagram earlier in the chapter for comparison.) The customer comes first and everything follows from that. I've broken the BMC's Key Resources block into two blocks: People, and Assets & Locations. I've also broken the BMC's Key Partners block into two blocks: Suppliers, and Key Partners. I've replaced the BMC's Key Activities block with a value chain, which I've labeled Value Creating Activities.

In using this template, the work done in populating the four blue boxes is not significantly different from the work done in populating the two corresponding boxes on the BMC, just broken down one more level. That additional step, however, I find really helps leaders think about the unique needs of their business.

The hardest work, however, is in defining the value chain[3] involved in creating and delivering the value proposition for customers.

What is a Value Chain?

MICHAEL PORTER INTRODUCED the concept of a value chain in his 1985 book *Competitive Advantage*[26]. Porter describes a value chain as "disaggregating a company into its strategically relevant activities." Given that it was introduced in a book on competitive advantage, it's not surprising that he saw it as a powerful tool for focusing on potential sources of competitive advantage.

Below is the model of a value chain that Porter introduced:

---

3.   https://www.isc.hbs.edu/strategy/business-strategy/Pages/the-value-chain.aspx

The value chain for any given business will be somewhat unique, reflecting the specific activities required to create value for customers. In developing a value chain for the Value Creating Activities portion of the Operating Model, I recommend considering the categories of activities identified by Porter, but identifying specific activities at a much more granular and specific level. What are the key activities involved in creating and delivering the value proposition and how do those activities fit together?

As reflected on the Operating Model template, developing a deep understanding of how value gets created in your business also uncovers the financial implications for the business.

How Is Your Cash Flow?

THROUGHOUT THIS CHAPTER we've been looking at different aspects of the question "how do you make money?" We've looked at revenue models, business models, and operating models, and along the way I've dropped hints about the linkages between those activities and cash flow, but now I want to focus specifically on how cash flows through a business.

Below is a diagram of what I call the "cash cycle" — the cash equivalent (in business) for the "water cycle[4]" (in nature):

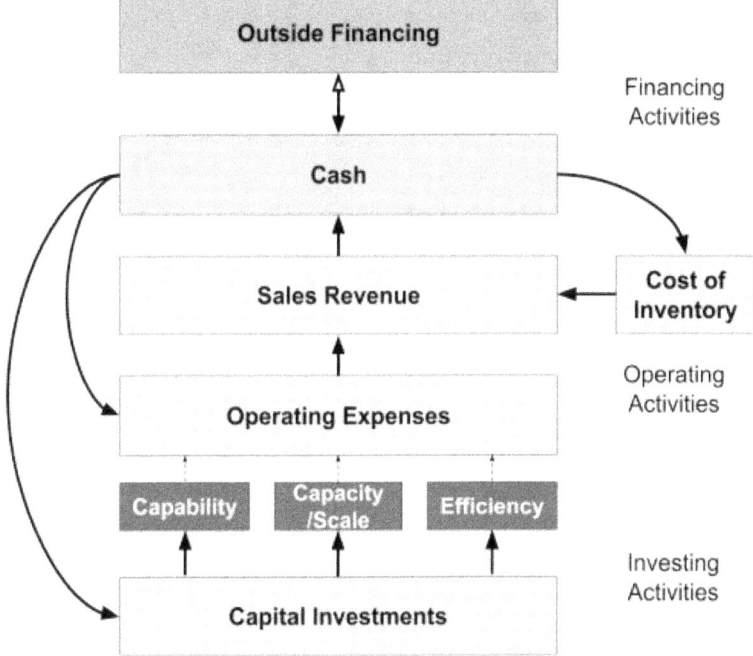

The business spends cash in three main ways: to buy what's needed to build the product or service you sell (Cost of Inventory), to pay for all the costs involved in running the business (Operating Expenses), and to make investments to establish capabilities, increase capacity, or improve efficiency in the business (Capital Investments). Hopefully all of these expenses contribute directly or indirectly to profitable sales (Sales Revenue), which replenishes the cash fund to enable the next round of spending.

When a business first starts, and likely at various times in the life of the business, managers may need to raise outside financing. That money comes into the top of the cycle to provide cash for various kinds of spending (especially capital investments). Depending on the form of financing, those providing that cash will likely expect a return on their

---

4.   https://gpm.nasa.gov/education/water-cycle

financing, so at times the business likely provides some of the business' cash back to those financiers. That might be in the form of principal and interest payments on a loan or in the form of distributions or dividends to equity investors.

There are a few important ways to keep an eye on the health of your cash flow.

Cash Conversion Cycle

THE FIRST ONE I'LL mention is the "cash conversion cycle" (CCC). I mention this one first not only because it's a helpful tool for managing cash flow health, but also because the CCC is sometimes called the "cash cycle", so some may confuse it with the "cash cycle" I've depicted above.

Unlike the diagram above, the cash conversion cycle is a number — specifically the number of days it takes for inventory to become cash.

The simple equation for the cash conversion cycle is:

$$CCC = DIO - DPO + DSO$$

DIO is Days Inventory Outstanding, which is the number of days on average that it takes to sell your inventory.

DPO is Days Payable Outstanding, which is the average number of days it takes you to pay your suppliers.

DSO is Days Sales Outstanding, which is the average number of days it takes your customers to pay you.

The longer your CCC, the more cash you need and the more of your cash that will be tied up in inventory. You can reduce your CCC by selling product faster (reducing DIO), negotiating with suppliers to pay them later (increasing DPO), or requiring customers to pay you sooner (reducing DSO).

Profitability

THE INCOME STATEMENT is the standard financial statement used to manage business profitability. It's important to understand that an income statement provides an *accounting* view of profitability for a specific historical period of time (typically a month, quarter, or year). Because of various rules for accounting, different revenue or expense items may be recorded in a different time period than when the actual cash enters or leaves the business. For example, accounting rules may require revenue to be reported when the product is delivered to the customer, even though the customer may not pay for it until sometime in the future.

Depreciation is probably the area where expenses are accounted for most differently than actual cash costs. For example, your business might purchase a desk for $600 and expect that desk to be used by the business for 10 years. Instead of reflecting a capital expense of $600 in the year the desk is purchased, the income statement might reflect $60 of depreciation in each of the 10 years of its useful life. That approach more accurately reflects whether the business is being managed for long-term profitability, but less accurately reflects the impact of the desk purchase on the cash position of the business.

Given those warnings, when I look at an income statement, the two main things I pay attention to are trends and margins.

Income statements are most helpful when compared to prior periods. What are the trends compared to the last few periods. Given that many businesses have seasonality (certain times of the year that tend to be stronger than others), for monthly or quarterly data it's also very helpful to look at the trends compared to the same period in each of the last several years. Are the numbers improving or getting worse?

Income statements are generally laid out to provide a number of important measures of profitability from top to bottom.

- **Gross Profit** = Sales Revenue – Cost of Goods Sold (roughly Cost of Inventory for the sales for that period)
- **Gross Margin** is Gross Profit as a percent of Sales Revenue.

- **EBITDA** (Earnings Before Interest Taxes Depreciation and Amortization) = Gross Profit – Operating Expenses (not including depreciation)
- **EBITDA Margin** is EBITDA as a percent of Sales Revenue.

- **Operating Income** (aka EBIT) = EBITDA – Depreciation and Amortization
- **Operating Margin** is Operating Income as a percent of Sales Revenue.

- **Net Income** = Operating Income – Interest and Taxes
- **Profit Margin** is Net Income as a percent of Sales Revenue.

When I look at a company's income statements, these are some of the important questions I'm trying to answer:

- Are sales increasing?
- What is the gross margin? Have they set their prices high enough to support the business?
- What is the trend on EBITDA margins? Are they keeping operating expenses in line with revenues?
- Are they profitable (Net Income)?

Cash Flow

THE CASH FLOW STATEMENT is the standard financial statement used to manage the cash position of the business. Unlike the income statement, the cash flow statement provides a true view of when cash enters and exits the business. Like the income statement, the cash flow statement reports cash flows for a specific time period (typically month, quarter, or year).

The cash flow statement has three main sections to report the different kinds of cash flows:

- The **Financing Activities** section reports cash flows into the business from investors (e.g. equity investments or loans) and cash flows out of the business to investors (e.g. dividends or loan payments).

- The **Operating Activities** section reports all forms of cash flows involved in operating the business (e.g. payments to suppliers, payroll, rent, payments from customers).

- The **Investing Activities** section reports cash flows related to investments made by the business (e.g. asset purchase or sale, mergers & acquisitions)

The important questions I try to answer by looking at cash flow statements include:

- Is the business generating or consuming cash?
- Is cash flow improving or getting worse?
- Is the cash flow from Operating Activities positive or negative?
- If operations are consuming cash (negative cash flow from Operating Activities), what is the monthly burn rate, and given how much cash the business has on hand (from their balance sheet), what is the runway (how long until the business runs out of money)?

As you can see, the question "how do you make money?" is a more complex question than it appears on the surface. Hopefully this chapter has given you a good sense for how to manage your business to make sure that you can answer the question with confidence for today and the future.

What Do You Need To Do Right Now?

W e've come to the last of the six questions that every business needs to be prepared to answer. What do you need to do right now? It can't be answered without doing the work of answering the first five questions.

Doing without understanding is like wandering in the dark. You're not likely to make meaningful progress. But understanding without doing is just as unproductive.

I suggest that in answering this question, we need to think about three key steps:

- Identifying what to do
- Doing the work
- Monitoring progress

Identifying What Needs To Be Done

IN MOST ORGANIZATIONS, there's plenty of work to be done, but how do we prioritize that work so that we're focused on those activities that will have the greatest impact?

I suggest that we look at three frameworks to help us identify the most important projects to start right now.

The Purpose Pyramid

MY FAVORITE STRATEGIC framework is the purpose pyramid:

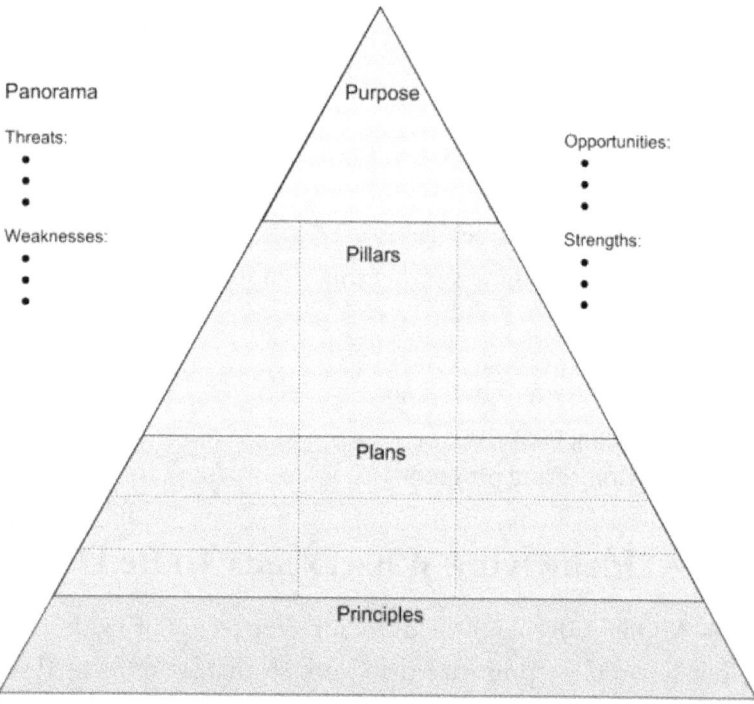

In this framework, the Purpose at the top is the "north star" that guides everything the organization is working towards. The question "why does your business exist?" defines the Purpose.

The strong foundation for this framework are the non-negotiable Principles that define how the business operates. The second question, "what principles will you never compromise?" provides the content for this part of the framework.

Below the Purpose are three Pillars — what are the three things that absolutely need to be true for the business to accomplish its Purpose? While we haven't framed any of the five questions to identify these pillars, it is likely that the work done in answering the questions "whom do you serve?" and "why do customers choose you?" will have uncovered the core elements necessary to support the Purpose.

It is these three Pillars that point to the work to be done. In the Purpose Pyramid framework, under each Pillar are three Plans. Once the Pillars are well understood, you need to ask the question for each — what do we need to do to firmly establish that Pillar?

The Customer Value Map

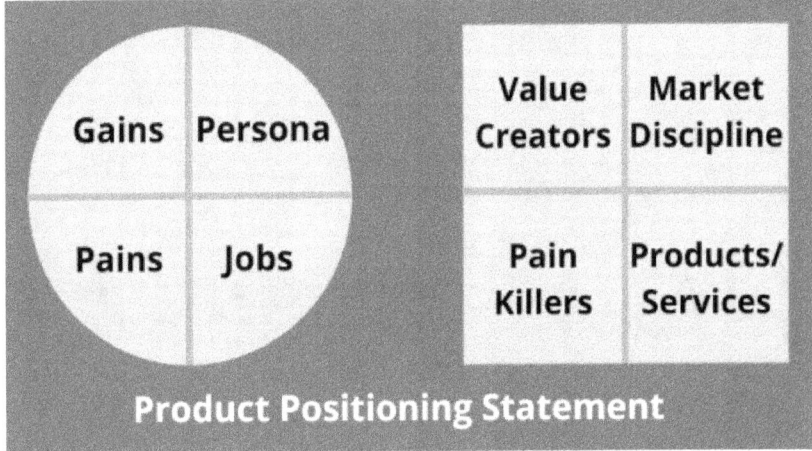

THE SECOND FRAMEWORK to help identify the work to be done is the Customer Value Map which I introduced in Chapter 5 on "Why Customers Choose You".

Based on our deep understanding of our customer, what can we do (in alignment with our market discipline) to increase the value created for them and to reduce or overcome their pains? These potential projects can further strengthen our value proposition and our differentiation.

The Cash Cycle

FINALLY, WE CAN EVALUATE work we could do to strengthen our cash flow. The third framework we can use to identify potential projects is the Cash Cycle that I introduced in the last chapter.

Are there things we can do to reduce our cash conversion cycle, to increase sales, or reduce operating expenses? Are there projects that would meaningfully add capabilities, increase capacity and scale, or increase efficiency?

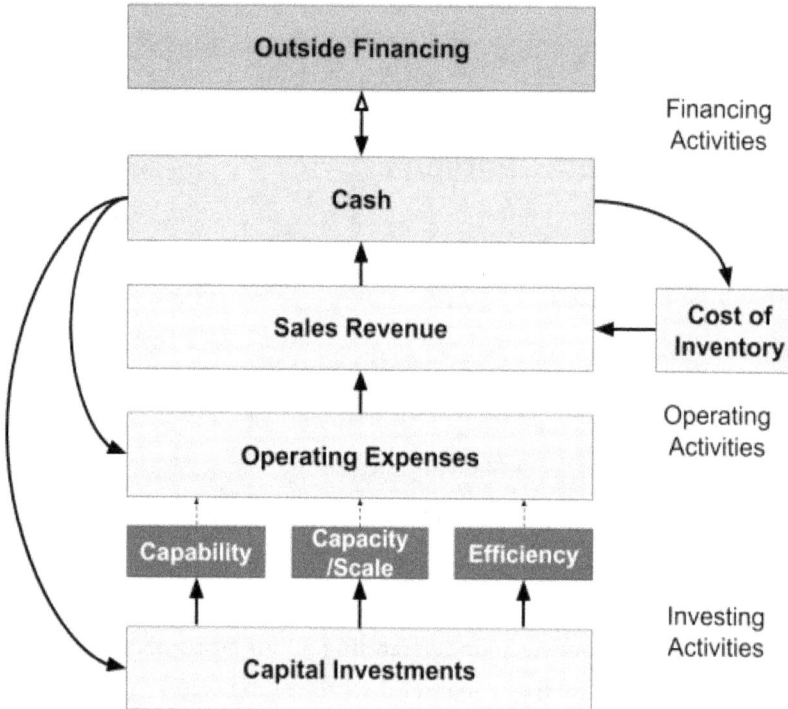

Prioritizing and Selecting

HOPEFULLY THESE THREE frameworks have helped us identify a robust list of potential work to do. But, there's a good chance we can't do it all, at least not right now.

Most companies have some sort of mechanism for prioritizing potential projects. This is often called a 1:N list, where projects are ranked from 1 to however many there are (N). Only so many can be done based on available resources (cash, developers, systems, facilities...). By ranking the projects, identifying the top ones that can be done with available resources becomes a straight-forward exercise. I recommend factoring strategic alignment, financial impact, and specific resources required into that ranking process.

So by using these three frameworks, we can identify work that could be done. By prioritizing those projects, we identify the most important work to get done. And based on the resources we have, we select the work that we will do.

Get It Done!

NOW WE NEED TO DO THE work. Major initiatives often involve change, which can be challenging to manage, and the specific nature of the initiative will impact how we think about and manage the work to be done. Specifically, I think it's helpful to identify which initiatives are starting something new, which are stopping something old, and which are enhancing an existing capability.

Start Something New

THE definition[1] of initiative is "an introductory step" and many initiatives involve starting something new. New ventures are almost always exciting and full of energy, but they can also be full of risks and challenges. Especially when launching something completely new to the organization, team members may lack the experience necessary to identify everything required for success. Because we tend to bring to

---

1. https://www.merriam-webster.com/dictionary/initiative

any new project perspectives established in previous projects, we may not even recognize as assumptions our beliefs about what will happen and how we can make it happen.

Tools used by startup businesses can prove helpful when launching new ventures within an existing organization. For example, the Validation Board, developed by Lean Startup Machine, provides a structured approach to identifying and testing assumptions that could potentially undermine your initiative.

[27]

Let's walk through the Validation Board process to get a feel for it in action. If you look at the Board, you'll first notice that it's split vertically. The top half is most meaningful for startup organizations and deals with hypotheses around the customer, the problem, and the proposed solution. For purposes of strategic initiative management within an existing organization, we will focus on the bottom half, which deals with assumptions.

The box in the bottom left holds a list of all the assumptions that the team can identify. Most teams go through three phases in developing this list. The first phase is when you struggle to identify assumptions, failing to recognize the things you take for granted. As Goldilocks might say "this list is too short". In the second phase, you go overboard and list things like "the world keeps spinning." Goldilocks: "This list is too long." Finally, you rationalize the list, eliminating the assumptions that are obviously too broad. ("Computer prices continue to fall" belongs on the list, but "computers continue to be manufactured" doesn't.) "This list is just right," Goldilocks might say. The Validation Board is a living document. As you continue to manage the initiative, you'll probably realize that there are more assumptions that you had overlooked. Continue to update this list as appropriate.

The next step is to identify the riskiest assumption. This is the one with the highest level of uncertainty and the highest impact on the success of the initiative. This moves into the Riskiest Assumption column.

The Validation Board process[28] involves developing an "experiment" to either validate or invalidate the assumption. That might involve doing research. It might involve talking to vendors or customers or other customers of vendors to learn from their experience. It might involve actually trying to do what you assume will work, but doing it in as small, fast, and inexpensive of a way possible to just prove or disprove the assumption. The "Method" box is where you describe this experiment.

For example, you may make an assumption that the next generation of a certain technology will be operated very similar to the current technology, not requiring significantly different skills, operations systems, or processes and procedures. The experiment for testing this assumption likely involves talking to vendors that sell the current technology and are likely to sell the next generation of it. By talking to several different vendors, you should be able to determine with a high level of confidence how much the operations will change for the next generation.

Before running the "experiment," you need to specify what you'll consider to be a success. What is the minimum level of performance that will meet the needs of the project — where anything less will cause the initiative to fail? This goes into the "Minimum Success Criterion" box.

Run the experiment, and based on the results, move that assumption into the collection of either invalidated or validated assumptions. Once done, move to the second riskiest assumption and repeat the process. To speed things up, you can work several assumptions in parallel. In reality, you don't need to test all of the assumptions. Before long you'll get to a level of assumption where the likelihood and impact are so low that they aren't worth testing.

Of course, as soon as you find an invalid assumption, you need to stop and determine how you are going to manage that situation. You effectively have three options:

- Cancel the initiative because it's no longer feasible.

- Update the initiative to reflect the newly understood reality. This may require returning to the planning process, understanding implications on other initiatives, updating the financial projections, and possibly again pursuing financial approval to proceed.

- Develop plans to mitigate the risk so that the assumption can be validated.

With the assumptions validated, implementation of the initiative can proceed.

Stop Something Old

STOPPING EXISTING ACTIVITIES may not be as much fun as starting new things, but you might be tempted to think that stopping is easier than starting. Often, that's not the case. Stopping one aspect of operations can impact customers, partners, and other parts of the operations, sometimes in surprising ways.

Before shutting down some aspect of your operations, make sure you have thought through all of the implications and have made appropriate plans. Sometimes, that planning can take years.

For example, in 2004, when Sprint and Nextel announced their merger, one of the largest blocks of financial synergy was expected to be cost savings from the shutdown of Nextel's iDEN network. The iDEN network was old technology with very limited data capabilities, but was highly valued for its push-to-talk (PTT) capabilities. The plan called for recreating the PTT capabilities on the Sprint CDMA network.

Unfortunately, the first attempts[2] to offer PTT on CDMA did not go well. The company wasn't able to have a version working well enough for customers until 2011, and even that version had significant limitations. The shutdown of the iDEN network became tied to a major upgrade of the CDMA network to overcome these limitations.

Finally, in May of 2012, Sprint Nextel announced[3] that the iDEN network would be decommissioned at the end of June 2013. It is unusual for a service provider to announce the shutdown of a service that far in advance. Usually, providers want to keep customers coming and paying for the service as long as possible, but Sprint needed to notify customers far enough in advance to give them time to smoothly switch to Sprint's CDMA network.

---

2.   https://www.cnet.com/reviews/kyocera-duramax-sprint-review/

3.   https://www.computerworld.com/article/2503730/sprint-to-shut-down-nextel-iden-network-next-year.html

For customers to make that switch, they also needed to switch phones. iDEN phones do not work on CDMA networks. Many iDEN customers were businesses with many phones that would need to be replaced. At the same time, all of the phone numbers needed to be migrated from the iDEN network to the CDMA network. Some customers only had iDEN phones and some had both iDEN and CDMA phones, and the customer and individual subscriber accounts had to be configured appropriately in all of Sprint's systems.

This transition was a huge customer and revenue risk for the company. When wireless users switch phones, they often consider whether to stick with their wireless carrier or to make a move to a competitor. Sprint was forcing customers to make that decision earlier than they otherwise would have. Nextel's PTT customers had historically been extremely loyal. Many were not happy with being forced off of the iDEN network that they knew and trusted. Getting these customers to stay with Sprint would be a challenge. For customers that had both iDEN and CDMA phones, the company risked losing all of the customer's business, not just the phones on iDEN.

For years prior to the shutdown, Sprint planned for how to work to retain as many customers as possible. Even before the official announcement, Sprint began working with its most valuable customers to try to retain them. This typically involved covering some or all of the cost of the new devices and offering steep discounts for service. In the end, Sprint was able to retain 44%[4] of its iDEN customers, which was considered a success.

Even when planned appropriately, shutdown efforts often will face internal and external resistance. Team members often rightly fear for their jobs when the product, platform, or function they support is being eliminated. Even if they can get reassigned, their skills and experience may be less valued than before. Good leaders are loyal to

---

4.   https://www.iphoneinformer.com/11500-sprint-sold-1-4-million-iphones-in-q2-loses-2-million-customers/

their people and may fight the shutdown decision, either actively or
passively. Managing through resistance will be critical to keeping
initiatives on track and on schedule.

A related challenge with shutdown efforts is what is often called
"pushing the bubble around." Shutdown initiatives are often based on
expected cost savings. The number of people and the costs associated
with a given product, platform, or function often appear clearly
delineated on a spreadsheet and the expectation is that those costs will
largely be eliminated. Unfortunately, oftentimes some of those costs are
actually allocations of costs associated with people and systems that
are shared across multiple products or platforms. Those resources are
still needed to support the continuing parts of the operation, so those
costs cannot be eliminated. Other times some of the people and costs
associated with what is being shut down can (sometimes legitimately,
sometimes not) move to other areas of the organization. Like squeezing
one part of a balloon to eliminate the air, just to have that air be
distributed to the rest of the balloon, eliminating costs in one area may
not actually eliminate costs from the entire organization.

Invest/Grow/Maintain Something Ongoing

SOME INITIATIVES INVOLVE implementing plans to change the
investment mix in the organization — defining where to invest and
grow and where to merely maintain the current position. In general
these types of initiatives are less complex and lower risk than those
involving starting or shutting down operations. However, when the
overall plan involves start-ups or shut-downs, these activities will
interact with ongoing operations in ways that impact timing and
sequencing.

For example, in the case of Sprint Nextel's shutdown of the iDEN
network, the timing of investments to grow the company's CDMA
platform were critical to the overall success of the strategy.

Sometimes, investments in ongoing activities must precede start-up/shut-down efforts (as in the Sprint Nextel case) and sometimes the investments must lag start-up/shut-down. For example, investment in an ongoing function may be dependent on the launch of a new capability, or the shut-down of an existing capability must be complete before the cost savings can be applied as an investment in an ongoing operation.

Managing and Monitoring Key Initiatives

OBVIOUSLY, INITIATIVES must be well managed to be successful. Project management and scorecarding are two mature disciplines that can play a significant role in ensuring initiatives remain on track.

Project Management

PROJECT AND PROGRAM management is a much larger topic than I can cover in this chapter, but below are some good starting points for how to think about managing a portfolio of initiatives.

The Boston Consulting Group (BCG), in a report for the Project Management Institute (PMI©)[29] identified four critical factors for successfully delivering on strategic initiatives:

- **Focus on Critical Initiatives:** Provide executives with a clear roadmap for each initiative that calls out a small number of critical milestones, provides explicit time frames, and identifies financial and operational metrics that are clearly linked to overall strategic objectives.

- **Institute Smart and Simple Processes:** Don't report too much information about each initiative. Doing so bogs down the teams executing the initiative and can confuse executives. Instead report on the overall performance of the program against targets, emerging issues that executives can help resolve, and the minimally sufficient information (e.g. just the metrics that are exceptions) to enable the executive team to actively participate in helping strategic initiatives succeed.

• **Foster Talent and Capabilities:** The PMI© has identified three critical skills for professional project managers: technical project management, leadership, and strategic and business management. Building a bench strong in these competencies will position your organization for long-term success in implementing strategic initiatives.

• **Encourage a Culture of Change:** Build organization-wide commitment to strategic initiative implementation as a real competitive differentiator.

Separately, in a report on connecting business strategy and project management, BCG and the PMI© introduced the concept of Benefits Realization Management (BRM)[30]. Three critical aspects of BRM are:

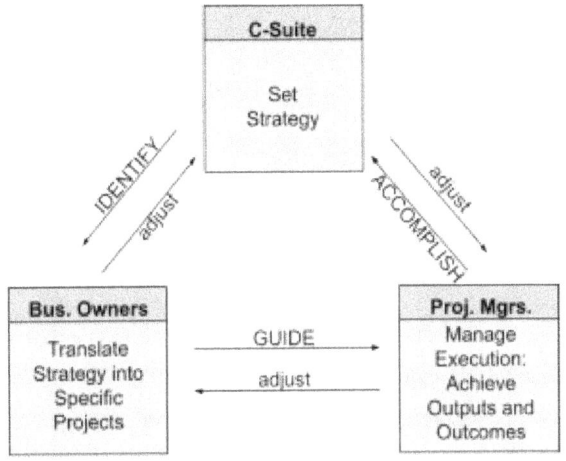

1. **Managing the portfolio of projects based on real strategic outcomes.** Traditionally, projects have been managed based on outputs, such as time, scope, and budget. Instead, focusing on outcomes (value, benefit, or utility) enables project decisions to achieve the real strategic objectives, even when outputs may miss their initial targets.

2. **Creating dedicated space for meaningful dialogue among C-suite executives, business owners, and project managers.** Typically the C-suite sets the strategy. The business owners translate the strategy into specific projects. The project managers manage execution to achieve desired outputs and outcomes. Without active engagement and shared responsibility amongst these groups, it is unlikely that strategic objectives will be achieved.

3. **Setting the right conditions for success, including establishing expectations regarding required behaviors, having the right project managers in place, and securing senior-level sponsorship.** These conditions are well summarized by the list of four critical success factors identified above by BCG. Two additional unfortunately common inappropriate behaviors identified include a "shoot the messenger" mentality by senior managers, making it unlikely that project managers will engage executives in resolving issues, which leads to "status watermelons" (a "green" status reported externally to executives, while the actual "red" status is kept internal to the project team).

Strategic Scorecarding

ALMOST ALL ORGANIZATIONS have regular performance reports that indicate whether the organization is hitting its objectives. Most organizations also have regular management meetings to discuss the performance of the organization and to initiate actions to correct performance issues. When asked about strategic monitoring, executives often point to these reports and meetings.

However, these typical performance monitoring mechanisms fail to ensure that the organization is on strategic track towards the desired end state in a number of ways as summarized below:

	Performance Monitoring	Strategic Monitoring
Primary Indicators	Lagging	Leading
Primary Focus	Financial	Capability
Monitoring Horizon	Current Month/Quarter/Year	Current & Coming Years
Resulting Action Plans	Reactive (Fire Drill)	Proactive

Don't get me wrong — regular performance monitoring is critical for any organization. If the organization is failing to deliver on current commitments, it may not survive to execute on the strategy. I just don't want you to confuse performance monitoring with strategic monitoring and therefore fail to be doing both.

In the early 1990s, Robert Kaplan and David Norton introduced their concept of the balanced scorecard[31]. They originally wanted to supplement traditional financial performance measures with those that indicate a company's progress in building the capabilities and gaining the intangible assets needed for future growth. The result was a management tool that reported performance through four lenses (which they called perspectives):

- **Learning and growth:** "To achieve our vision, how will we sustain our ability to change and improve?"

- **Internal business process:** "To satisfy our shareholders and customers, what business processes must we excel at?"

- **Customer:** "To achieve our vision, how should we appear to our customers?"

• **Financial:** "To succeed financially, how should we appear to our shareholders?"

By the time Kaplan and Norton wrote an article on the topic for *Harvard Business Review* in January 1996[32], they realized that the balanced scorecard was more than just a collection of metrics, but had become the core of a new strategic management system. "Recently, we have seen some companies move beyond our early vision for the scorecard to discover its value as the cornerstone of a new strategic management system. Used this way, the scorecard addresses a serious deficiency in traditional management systems: their inability to link a company's long-term strategy with its short-term actions."

In their 2001 book *The Strategy Focused Organization*[33] the pair explicitly laid out steps for implementing five key principles in their model for using the balanced scorecard to become a strategy focused organization:

1. Translating the strategy to operational terms
2. Aligning the organization to create synergies
3. Making strategy everyone's everyday job
4. Making strategy a continual process
5. Mobilizing change through executive leadership

At the core of linking strategy and operations is a tool that Kaplan and Norton call the strategy map. "A strategy map for a Balanced Scorecard makes explicit the strategy's hypotheses. Each measure of a Balanced Scorecard becomes embedded in a chain of cause-and-effect logic that connects the desired outcomes from the strategy with the drivers that will lead to the strategic outcomes."

Whether or not you are dogmatic about implementing balanced scorecards exactly as defined by Kaplan and Norton, I find the concept of strategy maps a great way to make sure that your strategy can be operationalized and that you are measuring the right things to ensure progress towards your desired end state.

Sprint Business Solutions

TO HELP SHOW HOW THIS works, let's consider an example. I joined Sprint in 2003 as director of strategic planning for one of the company's divisions at a time when Sprint was going through a major transformation. The company had been operating as three product-centric divisions (wireless, long distance, and local) and was reorganizing to customer-defined divisions (business, national consumer, and local consumer). I worked closely with the leadership team for the new Sprint Business Solutions to develop their strategy and plan.

The strategy is best represented by this Purpose Pyramid:

Panorama

Threats:
- Long distance in steep decline
- Mobility displacing wireline revenues
- Industry consolidation strengthening rivals

Opportunities:
- Fixed/mobile integration
- Voice/data convergence
- Voice over IP services collapsing local/long-distance/global calling

Purpose

Destroy Legacy Industry Barriers That Hinder Our Customers' Success

Weaknesses:
- Weak business wireless capabilities
- High last mile access costs
- Scale disadvantage

Strengths:
- Out-reach Bells, Out-wireless AT&T and MCI
- Strong assets for integrated solutions
- Strong base of business customers

Pillars

Deepen Relationships with Customers	Be the Leader in Wireless/Wireline Integrated Solutions	Be the Easiest to do Business With

Plans

Grow Share of Wallet in Base	Introduce Innovative Solutions	Make Loyalty Easy For Customers
Grow the Base	Develop Vertical Market Solutions	Shift Culture to a Customer Focus
Focus on Key Complementary Partnerships	Leverage Partners' Expertise & Products	Link Processes and Systems to Customer Impact

To bring this into a Balanced Scorecard perspective, we can recast this as a strategy map:

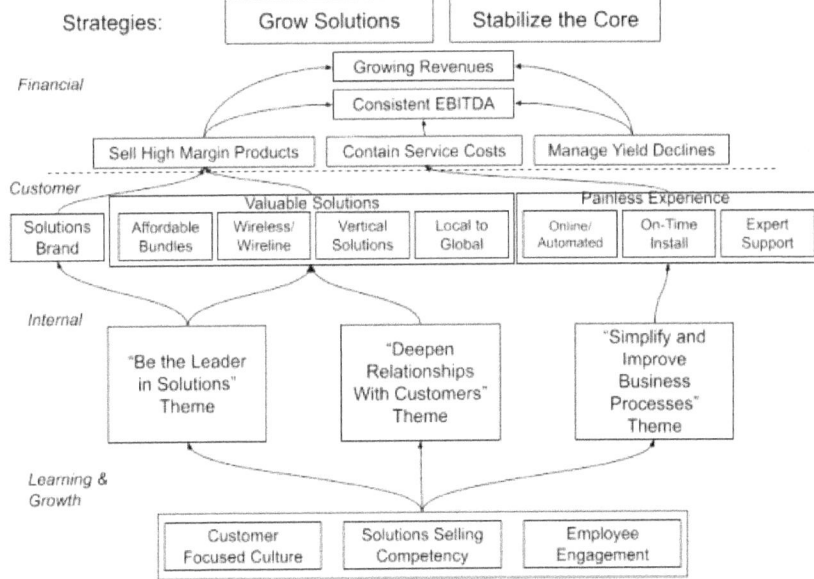

We can then specifically take the "Be the Leader in Solutions" theme and further develop the strategy map, the metrics for the balanced scorecard, and the key initiatives:

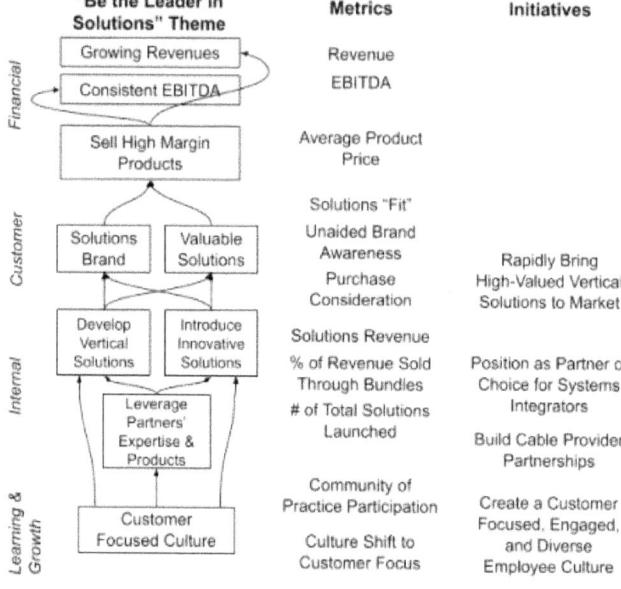

To manage our progress on these initiatives, my team developed a management dashboard with all the key metrics. We used this in a weekly meeting of the SBS leadership team and then in a monthly operations review with Sprint's CEO, COO, and CFO. Below is a representation of the dashboard from 2005:

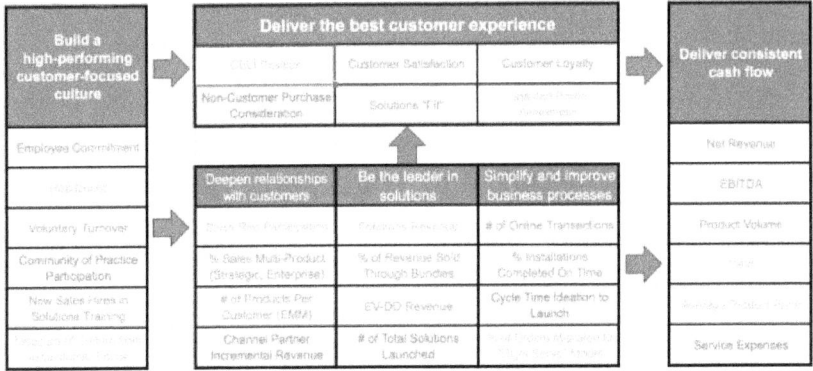

Regular Management Reviews

AS WITH ANYTHING, DEVELOPING a balanced scorecard is valuable only if you use it. Regular management meetings need to evaluate:

- **Execution of the strategy** — are we hitting the targets for our metrics?

- **Effectiveness of the strategy** — is the strategy producing the desired results?

- **Validity of the strategic hypotheses** — do the expected linkages reflected in the strategy map actually occur?

- **Confirmation of the strategy** — do changing conditions (internal or external) demand changes to the strategy?

- **Strategic initiative progress** — are they on track and producing the expected results?

When we talked about project management earlier in this chapter, we discussed the need to layout a roadmap for each strategic initiative with a relatively small number of critical milestones. Progress against these milestones is a natural topic for discussion in strategy reviews.

Also earlier in this chapter I called out the opportunity to identify and test risky assumptions and hypotheses for some initiatives. Learnings from these tests are also essential discussion topics among leadership.

Finally, as the initiative progresses, management will want to ensure that it is producing the desired results.

. . . .

AND SO, IDENTIFYING and prioritizing the right work, and successfully managing that work completes the sixth of our critical questions for business leaders.

The Six Questions Answered

Through the course of this book we've looked at six questions that every leader needs to be prepared to answer about their business. Along the way we've studied the business' purpose, non-negotiable principles, customers, competitive strategy, value proposition, business model, revenue model, operations model, and strategic initiatives. All simply by asking six seemingly simple questions:

1. Why does the business exist?
2. What principles will the leaders never compromise?
3. Whom do they serve?
4. Why do customers choose them?
5. How do they make money?
6. What do they need to do right now?

The questions may be short, and the answers may even be crisp and concise, but the work required to be ready to give an answer is far from trivial. In fact, that work, the lessons learned, and the direction provided are what make asking these questions so critical to the success of any business.

I hope these simple questions, and understanding what it takes to be prepared to answer them, have been a blessing to you. May you be blessed with wisdom, knowledge, and understanding!

[1] Collins, J. C., & Porras, J. I. (1994). *Built to Last: Successful Habits of Visionary Companies*. New York: Harper Business.

[2] Ibid.

[3] Sinek, S. (2009). *Start With Why: How Great Leaders Inspire Everyone to Take Action*. New York: Penguin Group.

[4] Battelle, John. *The Search: How Google and Its Rivals Rewrote the Rules of Business and Transformed Our Culture*. New York: Portfolio, 2005.

[5] Johnson, B. (2010, January 13). *How Google censors its results in China*. The Guardian. https://www.theguardian.com/technology/2010/jan/13/how-google-censors-china

[6] Thomson, J. (2018, December 18). *Company Culture Soars At Southwest Airlines*. Forbes. https://www.forbes.com/sites/jeffthomson/2018/12/18/company-culture-soars-at-southwest-airlines/#2b4e78c1615f

[7] Kotler, P., & Keller, K. L. (2016). *A framework for marketing management*. London: Pearson Education.

[8] Pride, W. M., & Ferrell, O. C. (2014). *Marketing*. Mason, OH: South-Western Cengage Learning.

[9] Blank, Steven Gary., and Bob Dorf. *The Startup Owners Manual: The Step-by-step Guide for Building a Great Company*. Pescadero, CA: K & S Ranch, 2012.

[10] Osterwalder, Alexander, Yves Pigneur, Gregory Bernarda, and Alan Smith. *Value Proposition Design*. Hoboken, NJ: Wiley, 2014.

[11] Ibid.

[12] Blank and Dorf.

[13] Kim, W. Chan., and Renée Mauborgne. *Blue Ocean Strategy: How to Create Uncontested Market Space and Make the Competition Irrelevant*. Boston, Massachuetts: Harvard Bus Review Press, 2016.

[14] 1 Corinthians 15:33 *The Holy Bible, English Standard Version.* ESV® Text Edition: 2016. Copyright © 2001 by Crossway Bibles, a publishing ministry of Good News Publishers.

[15] Yoon, E. & Deeken, L. (2013, March). Why It Pays to Be a Category Creator. *Harvard Business Review.*

[16] TeleChoice. (2002, March). Category Making in a Down Market. TeleChoice, Inc.

[17] Porter, M. E. (1980). *Competitive Strategy: Techniques for Analyzing Industries and Competitors.* New York: Free.

[18] Treacy, Michael, and Frederik D. Wiersema. *The Discipline of Market Leaders.* Reading, MA: Addison-Wesley Pub., 1995.

[19] Osterwalder, Pigneur, Bernarda, and Smith.

[20] Kaplan, Robert S., and David P. Norton. *The Strategy-focused Organization: How Balanced Scorecard Companies Thrive in the New Business Environment.* Boston, MA: Harvard Business School Press, 2001.

[21] Blank and Dorf.

[22] Moore, Geoffrey A. *Crossing the Chasm : Marketing and Selling High-Tech Products to Mainstream Customers.* New York, NY: Harper Business, 1991.

[23] Osterwalder, A., & Pigneur, Y. (2013). *Business Model Generation: A handbook for visionaries, game changers, and challengers.* New York: Wiley & Sons.

[24] Iansiti, M., & Lakhani, K. (2020). *Competing in the Age of AI: Strategy and Leadership When Algorithms and Networks Run the World.* Boston, MA: Harvard Business Review Press.

[25] Chesbrough, H. (2006). *Open Business Models: How to Thrive in the New Innovation Landscape.* Boston, MA: Harvard Business School Press.

[26] Porter, Michael E. (1985). *Competitive Advantage: Creating and Sustaining Superior Performance.* New York.: Simon and Schuster.

[27] Retrieved from https://www.leanstartupmachine.com/validationboard/

[28] Lean Startup Machine. (2012, October 01). "How to Use the Validation Board to Test Your Startup Idea". Retrieved from https://www.youtube.com/watch?v=HhoducyStMw

[29] Keenan, P., Bickford, J., Doust, A., Tankersley, J., Johnson, C., McCaffrey, J., . . . Shah, G. (2013, November 11). "Strategic Initiative Management: The PMO Imperative". Retrieved from https://www.bcg.com/en-au/publications/2013/program_management_change_management_strategic_initiative_manage

[30] The Boston Consulting Group (2016). Connecting Business Strategy and Project Management.

[31] *HBRs 10 Must Reads on Strategy.* Boston (Massachusetts): Harvard Business Review, 2011.

[32] Ibid.

[33] Kaplan and Norton.

Don't miss out!

Visit the website below and you can sign up to receive emails whenever Russell McGuire publishes a new book. There's no charge and no obligation.

https://books2read.com/r/B-A-NWOL-TYJJB

BOOKS 2 READ

Connecting independent readers to independent writers.

Did you love *Six Questions*? Then you should read *A Sprint to the Finish*[1] by Russell McGuire!

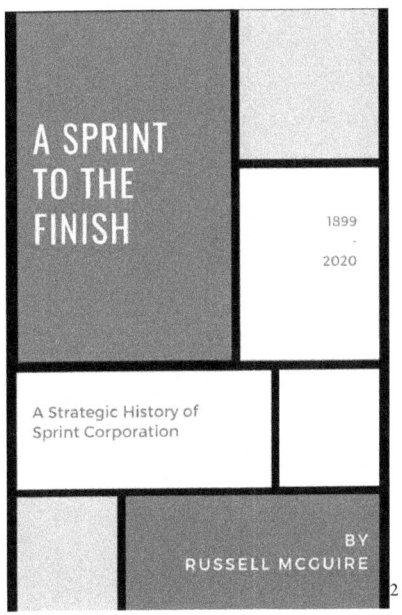

[2]

For over a century Sprint was an innovative leader in the telecommunications industry. From its humble beginnings stringing wires to homes and businesses in Abilene, Kansas, to helping build the global Internet, and stockpiling the richest porfolio of spectrum for fifth-generation (5G) wireless services, Sprint had an outsized impact on how everyday citizens and the world's largest companies communicate. Over those 100+ years, the company made a number of critical strategic decisions eventually leading to the final decision to merge with T-Mobile to become the second largest wireless provider in the country. Join us for an insider's view as we revisit this pioneering company's strategic journey!

---

1. https://books2read.com/u/38MJqO

2. https://books2read.com/u/38MJqO

Read more at sdgstrategy.com.

Also by Russell McGuire

A Sprint to the Finish
VisuALS: A Startup Strategic Journey
Six Questions

Watch for more at sdgstrategy.com.

About the Author

Russ McGuire is a trusted advisor with proven strategic insights. He has been blessed to serve as an executive in Fortune 500 companies, found technology startups, be awarded technology patents, author a book and contribute to others, write dozens of articles for various publications, and speak at many conferences. More importantly, he's a husband and father who cares about people, and he's a committed Christian who operates with integrity and believes in doing what is right.

Read more at sdgstrategy.com.

 **SDG STRATEGY**

About the Publisher

SDG Strategy helps values-driven leaders of tech-driven startups with the hard decisions they face everyday.

Building and growing a startup is hard. Technology is always evolving, but your values need to be grounded in the unchanging truths and priorities that guide your life. As a leader in a dynamic environment, everyone is looking to you for all kinds of decisions, and few of them are easy. Russ McGuire has been there. Russ brings tools, methodologies, skills, and lessons learned from working with dozens of technology companies over 30+ years.

SDG offers ongoing coaching, strategy lab workshops, online tools, and educational content. Visit us at http://sdgstrategy.com to learn more and to schedule a free 30 minute consultation.